IN FINGAL'S WAKE:
A TENDER TRIBUTE

In Fingal's Wake:
A Tender Tribute

Trevor Boult
with a
Foreword by HRH the Princess Royal

AMBERLEY

To my wife, Karen: another 'Fine-Gal'!

Front cover photograph:
Fingal on passage in the Sound of Mull. (Collection of Alan Provan)

Back cover images:
Collage depicting the work of NLB ships, created by the author while off-duty on *Fingal*.

First published 2016

Amberley Publishing
The Hill, Stroud
Gloucestershire, GL5 4EP

www.amberley-books.com

British Library Cataloguing in Publication Data.
A catalogue record for this book is available from the British Library.

ISBN 978 1 4456 4806 4 (print)
ISBN 978 1 4456 4807 1 (ebook)

Typeset in 11pt on 12pt Sabon.
Typesetting and Origination by Amberley Publishing.
Printed in the UK.

Contents

Foreword

BUCKINGHAM PALACE

As Patron of the Northern Lighthouse Board I have spent some memorable occasions on *Fingal* observing her work of ensuring that the coastal waters of Scotland and the Isle of Man are provided with the most effective and reliable aids to navigation, for the safety of all mariners.

The author pays tribute to this special ship which is widely held in affection and regard, not least for her sea keeping qualities which I also appreciated. Her future role as Scotland's first 'floating' hotel, adjacent to the former Royal Yacht *Britannia*, is a new and exciting development for this important example of Scotland's maritime heritage.

Anne

Introduction

Captain Eric Smith is a Senior Master with the Northern Lighthouse Board – NLB. He joined in 1986 as a junior second officer on *Pole Star*, which was an almost identical sister ship to *Fingal*. Captain Smith, together with his opposite-shift colleague, Captain Alan Rore, served as masters on *Fingal* throughout my own tenure as junior second officer. Captain Smith provides the following introduction to the operations of the tenders from the mid-1980s onwards to set *Fingal* in her historic context.

My first NLB ship was *Pole Star (III)*. At that time she was based at Stromness, in the Orkney Islands. Having completed my training and subsequent employment deep sea with a commercial shipping company, this was a big change. At that time there were three NLB ships in the service: *Pharos (VIII)*, based in Leith; *Pole Star (III)* at Stromness; and *Fingal*, stationed at Oban.

Pharos covered the area from the border to the Moray Firth; *Pole Star* tended Orkney, Shetland, and west as far as Skye and the North Hebrides; *Fingal* covered the rest of the west coast, including the Isle of Man.

The rota/leave roster was eight weeks on, four weeks off. There was a half-crew changed every four weeks, which required one-and-a-half crews per vessel. However, gradual automation of the lighthouses and reliefs of light-keepers by helicopter, rather than by sea, enabled *Pharos* to operate with just one crew.

The working pattern was mainly Monday to Friday with weekends off. The ships were in home port apart from attending lighthouse and buoy servicing as required. If the ships went out over the weekend, there was overtime payment for all on board. Due to this traditional work pattern, the majority of the crew were normally from the home port of the vessel they served on. It was not the case with the officers, as the majority had come from a deep-sea background with mainly Foreign Going certificates of competency. From time to time, officers were also required to move between the three vessels in the service. Although not a requirement, prior to my arrival many officers bought or rented property where they were based. Many ended up making their permanent homes there.

In 1986, there were still many manned lighthouses, with reliefs carried out on all bar one by helicopter, excepting the land stations, which were accessible by road. Bell Rock, off the approaches to the Firth of Forth, was still relieved by boat. *Pharos* carried out the boat reliefs during her eight-week operational period. During the subsequent four-week lay-ups, reliefs were attended by *Pole Star*, brought south from Orkney.

Boat relief at Bell Rock could be an interesting operation. My employment with the NLB started in late summer, and so the first relief I was involved in was in the autumn, with weather and daylight as factors. Normal routine was for *Pole Star* to dock in Leith or anchor off Granton to collect the keepers and their supplies. We would then proceed direct to the light or to anchor, and await suitable conditions. The keepers due off were keen to get the relief done and so, whenever radio contact was made, conditions at the landing were always reported as 'good'! Relief by boat was made on the ebb tide when the grating walkway from the base of the lighthouse was just visible. This gave the boat time to go alongside the landing, transfer the keepers and their gear on, and off, and then vacate the area before the danger arose of becoming 'neaped' by the run of the falling tide. This accomplished, it was then usually possible to transfer the keepers ashore at Arbroath by rubber dinghy before the tide there was too low.

In 1986, the crew size on *Fingal* and *Pole Star* was quite large: master, three mates, chief engineer, two engineers, boatswain, carpenter, coxswain, launchman, eleven seamen, engine-room storekeeper, three greasers, cook, steward, and two assistant stewards.

A lot of the deck work was labour intensive. When storing lighthouses, quite often both launches were used. There were crew ashore at the station to land the cargo; crew on the ship to work that side; and there were watchkeepers. During helicopter operations, crew were needed on board and ashore. Watchkeepers and a boat crew were required to stand by in case the helicopter ditched. Additionally, at that time, the ships were not fitted with autopilot. As helmsmen were therefore necessary on passage, there were three seamen on each watch.

Part of my duties as junior second officer was to complete the wage sheets. This involved recording all the additional duties for which extra payment was made at the time, e.g., night on board, weekend away from home port, cargo payment, 'difficult station' storing payment, etc. It was not long previous to this that my predecessors had to calculate tax, and make up the weekly cash wages. By the time I joined, nearly all hands were on a monthly salary.

Although the helicopter side of the work was interesting, it was always done fairly quickly: time is money. *Fingal* and *Pole Star* had been retro-fitted with a helipad aft and associated fuelling and fire-fighting facilities. The main helicopter task involving the ships then was the annual or bi-annual replenishing of acetylene gas cylinders at the lighthouses. Following automation and prior to solar and hybrid battery systems, this was the main power supply to many lights. There is always ongoing maintenance and refurbishment at the lights, which normally requires quantities of building materials and plant to be landed. This was also done by helicopter.

At manned stations, the boats were used to land diesel and water in sufficient quantity to keep the station running. This was done at a more leisurely pace than helicopter work and was only possible when sea and weather conditions at the landings were suitable. A steel tank fitted with a pump, and about a tonne of either diesel or water was placed in each boat. At some landings, such as Cape Wrath, Pentland Skerries and Muckle Flugga, there was a need for the workboat to lie at anchor and run mooring lines from both sides of the boat. This boat would then stay for the duration, with the other running a shuttle back and forth to the ship. At other landings, both boats would shuttle. Generally, such work took at least half a day. During the summer it was most enjoyable, the lightkeepers keeping us supplied with biscuits and hot beverages.

Another interesting but infrequent task at the lights was landing a tractor or a Land Rover. This was loaded onto the deck in port and taken out to the station. Here, both boats were launched and tethered together side by side. Hatch boards were then placed across the gunwales of the boats and the vehicle lowered onto this platform. At the landing, using planks and whatever else was available, a ramp was fashioned to drive the vehicle onto the landing pier.

The general method used in the inspection and maintenance of navigation buoys by traditional tenders like *Fingal* and *Pole Star* is the subject of a later chapter. These methods changed significantly with the introduction of the latest generation of tenders, where 'dynamic positioning' is used to approach a buoy and thereafter to keep the ship on station.

At the time I started with the NLB, the accommodations on *Fingal* and *Pole Star* consisted of single cabins for officers and double cabins for crew. The only en-suite cabin was the master's, who also had a separate dayroom and bedroom. There was officials' accommodation on the boat deck and accommodation for lightkeepers at the forward end of the crew alleyway, one deck down. There was an officers' dining saloon, and separate messrooms for ratings, petty officers and lightkeepers.

In 1987, *Pharos (VIII)* was sold and, in early 1988, the rota system changed to four weeks on, four weeks off. Crew size was reduced and terms and conditions changed. The ships were no longer 'day boats' and weekends in port became a thing of the past. Due to the reduction in crew size, the accommodation was altered to single cabins, still with communal toilets and showers. The lightkeepers' accommodation was modified to crew/commissioners' cabins on *Fingal* and crew-only on *Pole Star.*

Following the sale of *Pharos (VIII)*, and prior to the introduction of her new-build namesake replacement, *Fingal* became the 'commissioners' ship' and was used for their annual inspection voyages. A larger lounge was created to take a big dinner table, which was used during these voyages.

Pole Star was sold in 1993, after which *Fingal* moved from Oban to become the 'Stromness' ship. The new *Pharos (IX)* was based in Oban. Shortly afterwards, the helicopter facility was removed from *Fingal*, although the helipad structure remained. The work was then divided between the ships. *Pharos* became the helicopter ship, and *Fingal* the buoy tender. *Pharos* also had buoy-servicing capability and carried this out on the west coast, as and when required.

Today's modern tenders have moved away from the traditional 'three-island' design, with its more general and conventional propulsion and steering, to modern forward accommodation, working areas aft, and diesel-electric dynamic-positioning capability.

Preface

'Welcome to the Northern Lighthouse Board, Mr Boult. You will be assigned to *Fingal* as a second officer.'

I had been invited for interview at the headquarters of the Northern Lighthouse Board – NLB – at 84 George Street, Edinburgh; with anticipation and controlled nerves, I had crossed the threshold of this hallowed ground beneath a statuesque depiction of a rock lighthouse in miniature. Its smooth, white finish shone out from the backdrop of the cool, grey, dressed stonework of the surrounding well-proportioned frontage. To an observant passer-by, it is an understated and enduring symbol of the purpose of the NLB, enshrined in its motto, 'For the Safety of All'. Together with two other regional lighthouse authorities, its noble remit is to provide for the safe navigation of all mariners in the coastal and offshore waters of the British Isles. Its particular jurisdiction covers all Scottish waters and those of the Isle of Man.

I had maintained a professional coolness but, in fact, was doubly delighted at my appointment. Not only had I finally become part of an historic organisation that provides specialist safety services to fellow seafarers, but I was now also a serving officer on a unique and much-admired little ship: *Fingal*. She was the last of the classic motor-ship tenders in the service of the Lighthouse Authorities.

Like all her predecessors and successors, her designation as a 'tender' acknowledges the essentially caring role of these vessels; they maintain the many aids to navigation, which enhance not only the safety of all manner of shipping, but the very shores they transit or approach.

Fingal remains unique. The names of Lighthouse Authority tenders generally transfer from one generation to the next. In the NLB, *Pharos* and *Pole Star* now adorn the bows of the latest and most modern AtoN – Aids to Navigation – tenders. There has only ever been one *Fingal*. In the latter part of her distinguished career, she became the board's dedicated buoy tender. Primarily responsible for all navigation buoys owned by, or under service contract to the NLB throughout its extensive jurisdiction, *Fingal* also carried out other statutory duties as required. In the course of the yearly round, *Fingal* became a well-known and welcome sight. Her classic elegance always enhanced any Scottish seascape. Her fine lines and knife-edged bow spun a delicate marbled tracery astern, like mermaids' lace. Sea-kindly and graceful, she was yet a formidable workhorse, well able to withstand the excesses of weather that she might encounter on passage in the time-sensitive execution of her duties.

Replaced in the millennium year by the latest *Pole Star* – a vessel incorporating advanced technologies in line with current and future operational needs – *Fingal* was sold out of service to a private buyer. It was a privilege to be part of the delivery crew that sailed her to her new home,

(Author's Collection)

moored in the River Fal, in Cornwall. The ship, renamed *Windsor Castle*, was maintained to a high standard. In 2014, she was acquired by the RY *Britannia* for conversion into Scotland's first 'boatique' luxury hotel. Aimed at enhancing the RY *Britannia* experience, it also secures a fitting place for the former *Fingal* as a truly iconic and living example of Scotland's maritime heritage.

CHAPTER 1

A Flying Start

Travelling to join and leave ship is a necessary part of a seafarer's life, burdened and limited by the luggage that carries not only all his work attire but what passes as the paraphernalia of home life when off duty. Such journeys are accepted as a means to an end. Being homeward-bound generally seems the more pleasant.

The journey to join *Fingal* in late January 1999 filled me with boyish enthusiasm and expectation. It had several novel elements, which I anticipated being within the happy realms of the human scale. It had a wonderful destination – the Orkneys. There were two flights in small, propeller-driven aircraft. I began the journey in late morning, locking up home in broad sunshine. Birdsong seemed to hint of springtime. The short walk to the Tyneside Metro station still brought an ache to my back as it grew accustomed to the rucksack, my old and trusty tartan bag, sporting a replacement handle in white spliced rope.

How nice not to have been tiptoeing out in the chill darkness of the small hours to a waiting taxi, destined for an exhausting day on the railways, only to arrive at a destination of lesser appeal. The Metro journey to the airport was quiet, simple, pleasant – and cheap!

The tiny DASH aeroplane, evocatively called *Mountain of the Birds*, provided a flight from Newcastle to Aberdeen of charm and excitement, even to a seasoned traveller. Flying at less than half the altitude of a jet, the views over Edinburgh were laid plain: Arthur's Seat; Princes Street; the Royal Yacht *Britannia* in Leith Docks; the great sun-shadow of the Forth Rail Bridge, which itself appeared an incongruously thin, red thread; a model super-tanker at its terminal jetty; the county of Fife, bounded by

Forth and Tay and the sea beyond. Flying low over Aberdeen, the layout of the harbour and city centre also jogged the memory of past maritime associations.

Onward from Aberdeen airport, the little SAAB aeroplane was equally charismatic. Displaying an impressive acceleration, it had climbed rapidly. The single stewardess lost no time in efficiently issuing the score of passengers with afternoon tea. Crossing the wide Moray Firth, the sunset glowed beyond Inverness and the massing clouds. The stage was being set for the rugged romance that is the Orkneys. No sooner had our stewardess cleared away than we made our approach for landing. Eavesdropping on conversations close by, I deduced that NLB employees were aboard: Orcadian crew members coming home on leave from the tender *Pharos* at Oban, and three – including myself – destined for *Fingal*.

At luggage collection, a friendly face from the NLB depot welcomed me. Together with a seaman and the third engineer, we made up a foursome in the blue Transit van that then sped us through the damping darkness to Stromness. Our destination exuded the aura of a large rural village, neon-lit and in repose. There was no sense of urban sprawl or the industry of dockland.

Stromness has a dramatic location. The island of Hoy provides an imposing backdrop. Nearby are the enclosed waters of the great natural harbour of Scapa Flow. The town owes its existence to its own lesser harbour, named Hamnavoe by Norsemen. Huddled around this sheltered bay, the town's distinctive architecture and layout are responses to the demanding imperatives of the sea. Many houses that fringe the shore have their gables facing the harbour, separated by narrow closes, and with massive individual piers and boat slips.

The harbour proper is terminal for the ferry that plies the infamous Pentland Firth to the Scottish mainland. Facilities provide for fishing vessels, yachts and the fleet of charter dive-boats that frequent the notable wrecks in Scapa Flow. A vital location for an RNLI lifeboat, Stromness was also a strategic supply and support depot for the NLB, and a base for the tender *Pole Star*. During a reorganisation, her sister ship, *Fingal*, previously assigned to the mainland west-coast depot at Oban, was relocated to Stromness.

It was at the imposingly gated entrance to this northern depot that the van suddenly stopped. Beyond, a neat and well-lit forecourt led tantalisingly out along a short pier, lined on one side by a row of various coloured buoys. At the end lay *Fingal* – another grand little old Lady of the Sea: my latest new workplace, and home-from-home.

Seeing the lit-up ship at a glance from stem to stern, in her classic vintage style, I warmed once again to the theme of the human scale. The little gangway led downwards onto the main deck. Seconds later, a single companionway took me into the cosy warmth of her interior. A teasing and jovial welcome was forthcoming from the chief steward and his assistant. I was soon ensconced, and instinctively recognised that precious commodity – a happy ship, and a long history within her fabric. I felt *déjà vu* of another illustrious veteran vessel of a similar era to *Fingal*; but the Royal Research Ship *John Biscoe*, forever associated with the Antarctic, had been dismantled several years previously.

My cabin, within the ship's hull, was lined with warm wood-veneer and I noted the solid woodwork of the high bunk, the drawers beneath it and the navy blue settee, the desk and cupboards, the old-school radiator boxed in behind lattice metalwork, the restful-toned carpet and stout, comfortable writing chair; all these things reflected long and varied occupancy. Above the huge bathroom-sized sink, with its glass shelf and chromed holders, a period glass water jug added a sculptural elegance to complement the faultless glaze of the wide bevel-edged mirror, and its illusion to a wider space. Bakelite switches and round-pin sockets sat comfortably with their modern components. The warm candle-like glow of the tungsten bulbs from the various bulkhead lights completed the welcome. *Fingal* very soon proved to be a 'Fine-Gal' indeed!

CHAPTER 2

And so to Sea ...

It is a common feature of most professions that, for a newcomer, integrating into the expected role is a challenge, regardless of previous experience. In the Merchant Navy, there are many ship-types and specialist theatres of operations. Traditionally, for the most part, officers train and qualify in the deep-sea commercial trades, gaining expertise that could be transferred partially to other sea-going appointments. No knowledge or skill is ever wasted.

Navigating officers – a sub-role of their formal title of 'deck officer', which reflects the 'cargo' aspect of their employment – face their first challenge as a bridge watchkeeper at sea, getting to know the realities of the ship while on passage. It is a time for extra vigilance and guarded excitement: like it or not, you will be under scrutiny as an unknown quantity!

A traditional starting point for initiation is witnessing and taking part on the bridge in the pre-sailing preparations of all equipment and testing of systems with the engineers. The principles are broadly similar, but the detailed make-up of individual ships is often singular.

Elsewhere, the vessel was also being brought steadily to a state of readiness. On cue, stations were called fore and aft. I was assigned to the bow mooring party, in direct sight with the bridge. A mechanical growl from beneath the feet heralded the starting of the bow thruster's diesel engine, accompanied by a belch of fumes from the exhaust integrated in the foremast. Portable radios were checked, and the signal for 'singling up' the ropes was issued. The more remote mooring party aft was instructed by radio to 'let go'. A physical gesture of up-thrust arms from the bridge-wing sufficed for the remaining bow rope to be released and swiftly recovered inboard. To the linesman ashore, the philosophical parting comment was, 'we'll see you when we see you.'

Awaiting the all-important 'all clear aft' and keeping secure the bow 'spring' rope that led aft, gentle movement forward resulted in the stern lifting clear of the quay. Three short blasts on the ship's whistle indicated to harbour-users that *Fingal* was engaging propulsion astern, to the discreet tinkling of the telegraph. Making sternway, when the bow was clear to swing, *Fingal* pirouetted smartly to point towards the harbour entrance.

The entrance and the nearby Hoy Sound beyond it are places requiring local knowledge of the combined effects of wind and very strong tidal streams. It was a dramatic exit from the harbour, with a goodly speed already achieved in order to effect a bold and sharp turn to the west. My instruction began immediately, as Captain Smith quietly intimated: 'Avoid entering Hoy Sound on a strong ebb, with a westerly wind. There are up to 9 knots of tidal stream against the wind: not recommended!'

On this day, the tide and wind were in unison. On full speed, the ship was making an impressive 13 knots through the water but, for a while, it was only making 4 knots over the ground against the elements: time to take in the dramatic surroundings. Everywhere was superlative scenery.

Astern, the P&O ferry *St Ola*, which was outward bound for the Pentland Firth crossing to mainland Scrabster, made us a small convoy. The snow-peppered heights of Hoy to the south eventually opened the 1,100-foot sheer cliffs to reveal the Old Man of Hoy, seemingly diminutive in the further distance. Clearing Hoy Mouth, a westerly course was set towards Cape Wrath.

Fingal faced a substantial head sea, but she was about to demonstrate her true mettle. Her graceful hull lines were, for the technical, described as having a block coefficient of 0.53. She had a cruiser stern and

Hoy Mouth, Orkney, from a watercolour by Crispin Worthington. (Author's Collection)

Negotiating the tricky tidal narrows beneath the Skye Bridge. (Author's Collection)

knife-edged bow, which sliced cleanly through the onrushing parade of waves, maintaining for the most part a speed of 12 knots. She exalted in her sleekness, the flare of her bow dissipating spray on the downward plunges, preceded by twin snorts of compressed water up the anchor hawse pipes. On the upward heave, cascades from the fo'c'sle were flung off as wind-caught spindrift.

Temporarily sailing one-short, I was assigned the four-hour watch from midday, as opposed to the earlier 'eight-to-twelve' position. Cape Wrath was duly impressive, with squalls of force nine and spray to the mastheads, and we cleared with equal drama when rounding this significant headland at a mile's distance. The lighthouse headlands of Stoer and Rubha're came and went before dusk fell. In the gathering lee and moderating conditions, all became comfortable, as *Fingal* bowled past Rona and down the Inner Sound of Skye, anchoring in Broadford Bay. The well-experienced watchmen kept anchor watch in their turn through the night, with an officer on call. As I was to write home: 'how delightfully civilised!'

To conclude this first extraordinary day, I also observed that the bridge was 'compact and airy; the big windows offering a conservatory view. With such scenery and atmospheric drama, who could complain at having such an "office" to work in? Not me!'

CHAPTER 3

Buoyage Matters

Throughout her career in Scottish waters, *Fingal* played her part in maintaining and modifying an ancient tradition – the provision of buoyage. It is a global tradition that continues to evolve, as new technologies and materials enhance effectiveness and efficiency.

Navigation buoys are readily identifiable floating marks, fixed in strategic positions to aid the mariner in making safe and proper passage. They can be seen in navigable rivers, estuaries, and in coastal and offshore waters where a wide range of hazards may exist. Buoys complement other physical navigation aids such as fixed beacons, light-vessels and lighthouses.

Buoys were first used in the tidal estuaries of great rivers. Here, the depth of water, the strength of the river current and tidal streams, and the variability of deep-water channels precluded the use of fixed beacons and landmarks. The first written evidence of buoys being used in such a manner in European waters appears at the end of the thirteenth century.

It has been considered likely that the earliest form of marker was made of floating beams or timber rafts, anchored to the seabed by ropes. Such floats would have been of most use in the estuarial approaches to rivers, in order to guide the larger ships of the period. However, these floats would soon have lost their buoyancy, requiring frequent replacement. There was a need for a more durable buoy with reliable buoyancy.

One of the first records of airtight barrel-buoys dates from the mid-fourteenth century, in the area now occupied by the Dutch city of Rotterdam. These barrels were essentially wine and beer casks, fashioned out of wooden oak staves and modified for the marine environment. They were capable of bearing a strong mooring chain without weakening the structure, which could lead to leaks and loss of buoyancy. All surfaces were treated with tar and the whole girdled with iron hoops. In its moored position, the broad flat face would be uppermost. Under the water, the narrow apex with its stout securing ring enabled the buoy to withstand the tugging and chafing in choppy waters. The mooring chain of long, loose links had swivels at each end. The anchor was a weighted sinker, commonly a cube of hand-worked stone. From this early design, a double cone was developed. Known as a 'nun buoy', the extra height provided enhanced visibility and an elevated point to attach an identifying 'top mark'.

It was the advent of metal construction that eventually enabled techniques of buoy manufacture to advance. This was matched by the provision of support facilities: dedicated depots where buoys could be built, repaired and maintained; buoy yachts and, later, steam-powered tenders with specialist equipment for laying and lifting; and the inspection of mooring chains. Personnel were appointed locally to report buoy casualties and skilled men recruited for the buoy yachts, which were used to replace or move marks that had gone adrift or shifted by storms.

Metalworking technology at the foundries eventually produced completely watertight iron buoys, internally braced with horizontal and vertical bulkheads. Following these new methods of construction, in the late nineteenth century there was an enormous increase in stationing buoys, which could now be laid in deep and exposed channels. More were needed as the draughts of ships increased, meaning that even deep shoal waters became dangerous.

For several centuries, buoys were essentially day marks. They could not be seen in darkness or detected in fog. It was not until the latter half of the nineteenth century that sound-signal apparatus was incorporated onto buoys in key locations. These would assist mariners in fog, whether near a danger or making a landfall in poor visibility. A bell buoy would carry a fixed bell, surrounded by free-swinging strikers that were activated by the wave-induced motion of the buoy. Whistles, induced by the compression of air from the same motion, produced a penetrating high-pitched moan, capable of being heard across several miles in the right conditions.

The most significant development was the installation of lighting systems, powered by stored compressed gas. Initially, these were fixed lights but, as they could easily be mistaken for ships' lights, flashing systems were later devised. Given the buoys' remote and unattended nature, a highly reliable flasher mechanism was needed.

The original fuel of choice was compressed oil gas but, in around 1912, the Swedish inventor Gustav Dalen solved the problem of producing a flashing sequence. He used acetylene gas pressure to activate a diaphragm valve beneath the gas jet. In one unfortunate experiment, an explosion blinded Dalen. During his convalescence, he invented the Aga stove and founded the Aga company. It became a leading global supplier of lighthouse equipment.

After a way was found to stabilise acetylene gas, it became the cheapest and most reliable source of light power for buoys and 'minor' lighthouses. Individual codes of flashes were pre-set by screw adjustments to the diaphragm, its mounting and accessories. In recognition of the brilliance of Dalen's gas-flow control system, he was awarded the Nobel Prize for Physics. Dalen's sun valve and its more sophisticated photo-electric variants enabled an automatic buoy or beacon gas light to be switched off at daybreak and on at dusk, thereby conserving the stock of gas and extending the period between replenishments.

New sources of power for buoy lighting continue to be explored or improved. Today, the most common system is that of solar energy trapped by photo-voltaic panels and stored in batteries. Other systems include air- and wave-turbine action. Advances in bulb technology enhance reliability and reduce the amount of electrical power needed.

The eighteenth-century nun buoys proved suitable for the display of top marks, a desirable addition that further identifies the buoy and the character of its navigational purpose. They continue to form an integral part of many of the most modern buoys today. As metal buoys came into service, it was a simple matter to incorporate a top mark on an iron-lattice superstructure atop the main body of the buoy. In time, this superstructure carried progressively more equipment to aid the mariner.

Buoys also came to be painted in bright, distinctive colours: white, red, green, yellow. These enhanced identification of particular buoys, given local knowledge or their depiction on adequate charts. However, there was no uniformity to the use of these colours. The problems caused by different conventions of both top marks and colour led to many, and long-lasting, confusions. In turn, these led to a protracted search for international uniformity, culminating in the Maritime Buoyage System of IALA – which originally stood for the International Association of Lighthouse Authorities.

It was only in 1981 that all participating nations agreed to incur the expense of putting the two new IALA systems in place – a century after the Northern Lighthouse Board inaugurated the use of automatic gas lighting on buoys in the Clyde, on Scotland's west coast.

By the 1880s, it had become generally clear that a system of buoyage in which a ship was assumed to be making for or leaving a harbour would not be adequate for the increasing number of buoys, which were being laid to mark outlying dangers such as shoals and submerged rocks. In these wider waters, vessels were on passage and not necessarily either entering or leaving port. This dilemma led to the development of a compass-point – or cardinal – system of marking for buoys particularly in the open sea, as opposed to buoys dedicated to marking only the edges of channels.

The attention directed at the inconsistencies of buoy-marking in different regions took into account the improved durability and visibility of iron buoys, which had led them to being moored further out to sea. There had been a proliferation in the number of such buoys. The greater speed of steamships required rapid identification of marks and the correct orientation of the ship in relation to them. Without these, a navigator was liable to steam over the dangers that the buoys were set to mark. It also became urgent to agree on what flash sequences of the lights should be adopted for the 'port' and 'starboard' buoys marking the sides of navigable channels. Two distinct categories of buoy identification developed: one based on colour, the other on buoy shape and top marks.

In the mid-1950s, the forum of the International Association of Lighthouse Authorities was set up. It took many conferences to reach consensus. The complexities of factors and national traditions led the world to adopt two principles of maritime buoyage: System A, and System B, which differ in the use of port and starboard buoys.

System B applies to the Americas, Philippines, South Korea and Japan. All other areas are covered by System A, including Britain. The three General Lighthouse Authorities of the British Isles – the NLB, Commissioners of Irish Lights, and Trinity House – and vessels like *Fingal* in Scottish waters are charged with its upkeep.

* * *

Navigation buoys in Scottish waters are subject to a scheduled annual programme of planned inspection and maintenance, as part of ensuring reliability of this vital resource. Occasionally, this work is interrupted in order to respond to a confirmed report of a 'casualty' to a buoy in another area, such as an extinguished light, missing top-mark, or being out of position after a storm. Such casualties are given priority, and *Fingal* made round-the-clock passages at best speed to remedy such problems. Due to closer cooperation, casualties may be attended by ships of the sister authorities if they are nearer to hand, with consequent savings in time and expense, and reduced disruption to wider operations.

Buoys come in many different shapes, sizes and colours, particular to their purpose and location. They may be found literally a stone's throw from the quaysides of busy ports, such as Dundee or Glasgow, or as a remote solitary sentinel guarding a treacherous feature, such as Humla Rock in the wild

Atlantic-fringed waters of the Little Minch. They can range in size from the towering High Focal Plane buoys (which, in some cases, have replaced formerly manned light-vessels) to small glass-fibre units, which can be found in the approaches to the lesser harbours in the Orkney Islands.

A rare and poignant example is the *Royal Oak* Memorial buoy. This marks the war-grave site in Orkney's Scapa Flow of the *Royal Oak,* a British battleship sunk with great loss of life by U-boat torpedo in 1939.

Navigation buoys often lie close to some form of hidden underwater hazard, whether the shelving side of a channel, a menacing rock, or the remains of a wreck. Tending to such buoys brings vessels like *Fingal* into potentially perilous proximity with these unforgiving hazards. It can be exacting work to carry out maintenance in a way that does not compromise the safety of the tender and her crew.

In all cases where a buoy needed to be lifted onto the working deck of *Fingal,* a careful assessment of conditions was made for the expected duration of the work. This included the varying directions and strengths of the wind and tidal streams, changes in working depths of water and the influence of river currents. If necessary, the work was postponed until optimum or acceptable conditions prevailed.

When *Fingal's* new-build replacement, *Pole Star IV,* came into operation, she was the first NLB tender to be fitted with dynamic positioning – an advanced computer-assisted system of manoeuvring and maintaining a

Local authority mooring buoy in a busy harbour setting at Lerwick in the Shetland Islands. (Author's Collection)

Clear and present danger: a south cardinal mark guards the entrance to Loch Tarbert, Harris, in the Outer Hebrides. (Author's Collection)

A small glass-fibre buoy in the sheltered harbour of Whitehall, Isle of Stronsay, Orkney. (Author's Collection)

ship's position. This brought immediate and appreciable change to the way in which buoys were serviced. The traditional method for ships like *Fingal*, prior to being fitted with a bow thruster, entailed positioning the ship to windward, or 'up-tide', and letting go a bow anchor on the side opposite to which the buoy would eventually be worked. The tender then dropped astern with careful use of rudder and main propulsion – twin propellers controlled in the engine-room via telegraphed orders rung from the bridge.

As soon as the buoy was alongside, a steel wire rope was used as a lasso to throw over the buoy and slip some distance down the submerged mooring chain, before pulling tight on the main deck capstan. A seaman then stepped from the low working deck onto the often-slippery body of the buoy, attaching a pair of lifting hooks. The crane lifted the buoy and its trailing mooring-bridle, sitting the buoy body squarely and upright on the deck. Sufficient chain was progressively hauled inboard, before being 'stoppered' securely at the ship's side. The visible working part of the chain was then gauged with callipers to assess the extent of wear since the last inspection. Depending on the results, lengths of chain could be 'end-for-ended', or replaced altogether from stock carried on board. This required lifting the entire mooring and its heavy sinker onto the deck.

Fingal was fitted with a diesel-powered azimuthing bow thruster midway through her career. This brought added manoeuvrability to the ship,

Attending local buoyage in Stromness Harbour as charter dive-boats head for Scapa Flow. (Author's Collection)

Idyllic conditions prior to replacing a 'safe water' position buoy in the outer approaches to Inverness. (Author's Collection)

Casting the wire 'lasso' to hold the buoy alongside. (Author's Collection)

Connecting the lifting strops. (Author's Collection)

Re-deploying the port-hand buoy off Arnish Point at the approach to Stornoway Harbour. (Author's Collection)

Hauling the mooring chain inboard with the capstan. (Author's Collection)

Bosun Mervyn Manson. (Author's Collection)

'Stoppering' the recovered chain to secure it on board. (Author's Collection)

Ship's carpenter, Alan James, gauges the wear on the working part of the chain. (Author's Collection)

The foredeck, cluttered with a variety of buoys for refurbishment at the depot. (Author's Collection)

enabling her to change heading and move slowly in any direction. Now, a buoy could helpfully be approached bow-on, without the complication of having to use an anchor that, on recovery, could snag the mooring of the buoy itself.

As soon as a buoy was landed, the team allocated to maintenance of the buoy body secured an aluminium ladder for access to the superstructure above by the inspecting officer on duty. A typical solar-panelled buoy would have the voltages of each panel and battery checked. A light-obscuring gloved hand or enshrouding black bin-bag created a false darkness to cause the light to begin flashing, at which time its characteristic timed sequence, or phase, was checked: for instance, a group of three quick white flashes for an East Cardinal mark; or a group of nine similar flashes for a West mark – a convention of recognition aided by the comparable hours of a clock face.

The general condition of any top-mark and the whole optic was inspected. The magnifying prismatic cover, able to focus and project the light from a mere 15 watts of power, would be tinted appropriately: clear, red, green, amber-yellow.

Some acetylene buoys were still in use at the close of *Fingal's* career, requiring the continued on-deck carriage of gas cylinders, spares, tooling and expertise to keep this old and venerated technology working. The gas cylinders, which were located in watertight pockets within the buoy body, lasted for twelve months. Each service required the changing of four to twelve cylinders.

On deck, crew would take up implements not dissimilar to the fighting quarterstaffs of medieval times. In reality, the long-handled scrapers, with their business-ends newly sharpened, attacked the marine growth that had attached itself to the lower parts of the buoy and its skirt. It was a noisy and wet operation, as fronds of seaweed and heavy encrustations of mussels cascaded to the deck, crunching loudly underfoot. Adjacent, the mooring chain received attention.

On the bridge, the captain and watch-keeping officer observed from their elevated position; extra pairs of eyes that kept an overview on the cluttered proceedings, as well as what was happening elsewhere, ready to react to changing conditions or the movements of other vessels. From the deck, a heavy rhythmic clamour accompanied the work of Mervyn the Bosun. Busy clenching a new length of chain to the North Lady buoy on Tayside, he expertly wielded the sledgehammer to the shackle-pin, preheated to malleability by blow-torch. Calling down from the bridge-wing, Captain Rore enquired, 'Is it me or the Mate you're thinking of when you're hitting that?' Throughout, in the engine room, the duty engineer and motorman remained patiently and attentively on standby at the controls.

Pots of brightly coloured paint appeared from the locker. Depending on condition, the buoy was given an appropriate level of repainting. Drips inevitably fell. Over time, their accumulation on the steel deck created a veritable and honest abstract worthy of many a contemporary art exhibition.

On completion of servicing, the buoy was made ready for redeploying. Where the complete buoy and mooring had been brought inboard for particular maintenance, or to remove the ship to a safe distance from immediate hazard, the tender needed to return to the charted position of the buoy. Latterly, this has been made simpler by the use of satellite GPS – Global Positioning System. Historically, determining the correct position has involved a local and hands-on approach, involving the use of the sextant in accurately measuring horizontal angles of fixed and readily identifiable reference points.

Bearings and distances from prominent landmarks, and scrutiny of good topographical radar targets were also used. As with many procedures in the NLB, there is 'The Book', with the positions of each and every buoy.

This not only details the latitude and longitude, but also contains numerous notes and annotations added during the years. Local marks and transits – recognisable features brought into vertical alignment – offer the most reliable visual references. All the information was considered in order to agree a position. Depending on weather and tide, the vessel might have been moving when the buoy was slipped, making it a judgement call by the Master.

Prior to the buoy being craned back into the water, the exposed mooring was carefully manhandled with chain-hooks into flakes on the deck. Poised with sledgehammer at the ready and with the deck party otherwise standing clear of danger, when given the thumbs-up sign from the bridge, the heavy stopper that hitherto had held the cable secure was struck a resounding blow. Instant reverberating cacophony ensued, as the weight of the chain accelerated and thundered overboard. As the mooring tautened and the final rope-tether was cleaved with a sharp axe, it snatched the buoy away from the ship in a fizzing turmoil of marbled water. All became quiet again as the thumbs-up all-clear sign was returned to the bridge.

As *Fingal* pulled away from her erstwhile tether of a buoy, free once more to manoeuvre, the deck party would set to, cleaning away the accumulated detritus of marine growth laboriously removed from the last buoy. The rasping shovels marshalled and dispatched the myriad mussel shells overside, aided by the powerful cleansing sweep of hoses. On completion, with the machinery also set at rest, the Bosun would signal to the bridge 'finished on deck', with the customary exaggerated mime of slicing a decisive finger across his throat, before joining his colleagues in the mess room. On the bridge-wing, the telegraph to the engine room would ring sweetly 'Full ahead', as the bridge watchkeeper resumed his navigational duties in the 'nervous centre'. The engineers below, released from standby, continued their business in the 'mechanical garden'.

The accurate placement of a navigation buoy can take into account both geographical and local considerations. On Scotland's west coast, Ardnamurchan Point is internationally respected and popularly considered as the dramatic westernmost extremity of the British mainland. The tip of the peninsula is marked by an equally well-known lighthouse, which guards the seaward end of the Sound of Mull. North of Ardnamurchan, a buoy marks Bo Faskadale Rock and, by inference, Elizabeth Rock a mile closer inshore. By necessity, the buoy's 40-cwt sinker needs to be placed with considerable accuracy in 50 metres of water on a narrow, steeply shelving neck, with considerably deeper water on either side. Its mooring chain is some 110 metres in length.

In the sheltered waters of Stromness Harbour, when *Fingal* replaced a buoy with a new-generation solar-powered type, its particular placement was to the requirements of local users – the ferries, fishermen and dive-charter boats. Illustrated in a photographic record compiled by the ship, its position is described as 'a line extended outwards from the face of the ferry pier, to intersect when the house on Inner Holm white flagpole aligns with the third window from the right-hand end'.

On occasions, conditions of perfect calm exist. These, however, can be both deceptive and potentially dangerous for buoy-maintenance work. With neither wind nor tide to lean into, the decision as to which side of the ship to work a buoy on deck can be arbitrary. During this vulnerable period, in the event of a marked change in external conditions, the vessel may inexorably be forced to swing in a direction contrary to safety.

Confirmed reports of a buoy casualty, often relayed from the NLB's headquarters in Edinburgh, can initiate much fresh activity aboard ship. The vessel's immediate plans and projected schedule are shelved to accommodate the need to address the new priority. This can involve steaming a considerable distance, almost regardless of weather conditions or the anticipated movements of personnel to or from periods of leave. It can also promote the quick and creative use of local resources to effect repair to a buoy already close to hand.

Fingal's comprehensive suite of conventional Admiralty paper charts were permanently latticed with many carefully assessed and neatly delineated passage plans. This aided the ship's ability to conduct her business quickly and efficiently throughout her extensive and complex jurisdiction. An entry in the author's journal for February 1999 recalls the early part of a particular response:

Anticipated a day/night alongside at Stromness, following completion of inspection work around the Orkneys. A sudden change, as the vessel is advised of a buoy casualty in the Firth of Forth: Inchkeith Fairway buoy, which marks the seaward end of the main approach channels, has an inoperative RACON radar responder beacon. Chief Engineer, who lives in Stromness, heard the tell-tale short blast of the whistle being tested, and sighted the radar scanners in motion. The Second Engineer from Cork, and Second Officer from Stornoway, realise that the following day's leave travel arrangements will be made less certain. The vessel is alive with purposeful preparations for sea ...

An unorthodox and creative solution was applied in response to a report by Oban Coastguard that Lochy Flat South buoy, off the Highland town of

Fort William at the head of Loch Linnhe, was exhibiting an irregular light. As *Fingal* was fortuitously alongside at Oban depot:

> I am dispatched ashore, with seaman Iain MacNee and some equipment, to be driven by Blair from depot to Fort William. On arrival, a dubious-looking inflatable boat is hired from a local waterfront business. The massive bulky backdrop of Ben Nevis is unseen in the heavy low cloud, as we gently traverse the oily-smooth waters of the loch, dimpled with raindrops. New lantern fitted to the buoy; all voltages checked, etc. On the way back in the car, a question nagged, against the prospect of professional embarrassment: 'have we remembered to do everything on the buoy?' Such questions are evidently normal. (Author's journal)

I had an unexpected greeting from the captain on my return from leave, who instructed me forthwith to man *Fingal's* fast but diminutive inflatable boat and to proceed from Stromness south to Clestrain Sound – the northern approach to Scapa Flow. There, I was to attend Riddock Shoal port-hand buoy, which had developed a systems fault. Orcadian seaman Clinton Marwick had made all preparations for our quick departure when I was properly attired.

It was to be an exhilarating, drenching, and shivering experience – akin to a mischievous terrier being let loose on a sandy foreshore. What appeared from deck height as an inviting early-spring jaunt on the sun-glistening waters of the Sound turned out to be an invigorating test against the elements, particularly on the return. The small-boat tactics of finding a lee from the wind, and making dog's-leg courses to turn the waves and tide-race to advantage, eventually brought the glow of recollected boyish satisfaction, as the feeling slowly returned to numbed hands and wind-chapped faces.

There are many sightings of unexpected and mysterious floating objects at sea, some of considerable hazard to shipping, or smaller craft. In the Shetlands, while carrying out scheduled operations in the Lerwick area, the trill of *Fingal's* cell phone brought a call from headquarters. The Scottish Fisheries Protection vessel *Vigilant* had sighted a drifting green can-buoy between the Orkneys and Fair Isle, to the north. It was evidently a small, private mark, of unknown origin.

Several days later, while on passage, serendipity – also an occasional uncanny feature of maritime life – intervened:

> About 10 miles SW of Sumburgh Head, the earlier-reported buoy was spotted on the port bow. Its unexpected and dark triangular appearance, plus the

solitary gull perched on top, gave a lurch to the navigational stomach ... It looked like a rock. Out here there should be no rocks! Confidence was soon recovered, and replaced with quiet satisfaction, as binocular scrutiny revealed it not only to be a floating object, but the wayward mystery mark.

'Action Stations!' – within minutes it was alongside, grappled and decked. Inspection revealed it to be a port-hand buoy, number 1497. Yet it was green in colour. Deduced as an IALA System B buoy, it evidently originated from the Eastern seaboard of North America; owned by the Canadian Department of Transportation. It had drifted some sixty miles in the four days since it was first reported.

Consisted: an intact battery box with trailing umbilical of wiring, and broken bridle chains. The top structure long demolished during its Atlantic crossing. The base of the weighted skirt was evidently ice-damaged – not hidden by the marine growth.

It had become a resting-place for a handful of gulls. They were inclined to boldness and landed on the deck to grab the loosened molluscs; a one-legged black-back gull dominating the gleaners. (Author's journal)

Some buoys have rare additional functions; a focal point beyond that of satisfying navigational needs. One such, a starboard-hand mark, bears the stout name 'Royal Oak'. Located in the north-eastern part of Scapa Flow, it carries a white plaque that states:

This marks the wreck of HMS *Royal Oak* and the grave of her crew. Respect their resting place. Unauthorised diving prohibited.

As with other major marks, it is subject to annual maintenance and four-yearly replacement. In July 1999, *Fingal* loaded a newly refurbished Royal Oak buoy at Stromness. Prior to being laid, the young Orkney crewman, Clinton, respectfully transferred the wreath and long-dried carnations from its predecessor to the new buoy's superstructure.

At Remembrance Day in the following November, a 'maroon' was fired at Stromness Harbour as part of the sixtieth anniversary of the sinking of *Royal Oak*. In an annual ceremony, Royal Navy divers place a White Ensign underwater at her stern.

CHAPTER 4

Taking to the Boats

The use of boats and launches in the work of Lighthouse Authority tenders has always been of fundamental importance. The variety of tasks to be carried out often places heavy demands on the skills of coxswains and crews alike. Some of the traditional roles have passed into history, particularly the regular storing and relief of manned lighthouses, which have long since been automated, and today may be visited, if required, by helicopter. Nevertheless, boatwork remains a frequent part of the modern service, with new-generation craft where traditional skills are still needed to ensure the safety of personnel.

Although specialist vessels, Aids-to-Navigation tenders are also merchant ships and, as such, are subject to many statutory regulations. The Convention of Safety of Life at Sea – SOLAS – stipulates the appliances necessary for the safe and proper evacuation of a ship at sea. These include design-approved lifeboats, which also need to be maintained and operated, and the crews exercised on a regular and official basis.

Fingal's main workboats were heavily constructed in wood, powerfully engined and fitted with quick-acting dodgers to provide proper protection in adverse operating conditions. The davit arrangements were designed for the frequent and rapid lowering, and the raising and securing of each boat, so as to minimise the hazards inherent in such operations. An inflatable craft with outboard engine was used for lighter duties, capable of higher speeds in sheltered conditions, and was handled by the ship's crane.

Due to structural additions made to *Fingal* for modified operational purposes, the two original SOLAS lifeboats were kept so as to maintain the ship's stability. The traditional 'luffing' davits – by which each boat was

Fingal's starboard lifeboat being exercised at 'Abandon Ship' drill. (Author's Collection)

The much-used workboats received frequent maintenance. (Author's Collection)

held, or suspended over the side during embarkation – had a lower centre of gravity than the faster-operating and more modern gravity davits, which necessarily had to sit higher in the stowed position. The luffing davits' lower placement provided a more pleasing aspect to the ship's profile, but needed not-inconsiderable manpower to move the davits by manual-mechanical means: an added bonus to the regular 'Abandon Ship' drills!

* * *

A common use of the launches is in response to buoy casualties, where a faulty component might be put right with the buoy *in situ*; a much simpler operation than landing a buoy aboard ship. Weather and sea conditions at the location are the main considerations. All standard navigation buoys are substantial structures when viewed from the sea-level deck of a launch. Their movement in a seaway becomes self-evident on approach, and it is prudent initially to stand off and assess the effects of swell, the run of the tide and the often-conflicting effects of wind waves.

On deciding the best approach, the coxswain generally 'stemmed' the dominant influence and brought *Fingal's* heavily fendered launch alongside. If appropriate, a loose securing was made to a lifting lug on the buoy. The gently convexed top of the buoy, so shaped to shed water, is often slippery-smooth with sea water, and even augmented by nauseous and slimy guano accretions from shags or cormorants taking advantage of a convenient and safe roost. These are some of the hazards for the first step on disembarking the launch, which, in its own individual movement, could crush the ankle of the unwary. The vertical latticed 'wings' of the buoy superstructure provide an excellent handhold for the officer and assisting crewman to carry out investigations. For comfort, the launch could stand off close by, so as to render further assistance as required.

A buoy's light may be extinguished, whether from a broken bulb, or batteries run down from lack of solar-charging in a prolonged spell of overcast winter weather – an initial problem very largely overcome by both greater charging and storage capacities. An acetylene light might need 'decoking', or adjustment to reinstate the correct flashing sequence, or a small emergency gas bottle rigged to supplement the remaining supply of acetylene prior to full replacement aboard ship. A storm-damaged topmark may need repair, or electrical connections made good to a radar responder beacon.

The open-sea approach to the Firth of Tay and to the port of Dundee is marked by the Abertay High Focal Plane buoy, a very substantial seamark as befits its status. It loomed high above the attending launch and had a

Seaman Clinton Marwick and Second Officer Donald MacLeod obscure a light sensor to activate a flashing light on a 'starboard-hand' buoy marking the seaward approach to Skye Bridge. (Author's Collection)

Effecting *in-situ* repair to Cromarty Fairway buoy. (Author's Collection)

boisterous white froth of tide harassing its skirts. Beneath and unseen, a lengthy counterbalance extended deep down in the water. One of the buoy's vertical solar panels, on a hinged door, had received irreparable damage; the whole needing replacement.

The statutory annual inspection of navigation aids provided by ports, harbours and local authorities is made possible by the use of the NLB's small craft. *Fingal's* launches were dispatched into a wide range of environments, from the northern outposts of the Shetlands to the Isle of Man, and the harbours of south-east Scotland to the Atlantic coasts of the Outer Hebrides.

On occasions, a launch was used to land personnel going on leave, and to collect their reliefs; or for logistic storing of minor stock or items of special equipment. Bustling harbours such as Aberdeen were negotiated from outside their entrance breakwaters to the landing steps at the innermost jetties. These were crowded with the supply ships and anchor-handlers of the oil trade, and also hosted the graceful lines of the ferry *St Sunniva*, preparing for her overnight passage to the Northern Isles. Remote and lesser harbours, too, have known the handshakes between colleagues as they head for home by convoluted and protracted means.

A High Focal Plane buoy at the outer approaches to the River Tay, eastern Scotland. (Author's Collection)

Robert (Big Rab) Longridge, launch crewman. (Author's Collection)

In Oban Harbour, off the NLB pier, Sean Rathbone and Donald MacLeod carry out a depth survey using one of *Fingal's* workboats. (Author's Collection)

A comparatively rare event saw a launch being adapted to carry out in-house hydrographic survey work for the development of the NLB's own pier at Oban. In anticipation of the next generation of ships, plans for the modification of the depot's facilities, both onshore and at the pier, were underway. The current depths of water and general profile of the seabed adjacent to the face of the pier, and its proposed extension, were a necessary adjunct. Equipment for the task was assembled on the launch, both the overside hardware, and the recording equipment strapped to the foredeck. In the busy confines of this part of Oban harbour, known locally by mariners as the 'Triangle of Tranquillity' because of its sheltered position, the launch made her careful and controlled transits. These were cheek-by-jowl with berthing fishing boats, pleasure craft and the frequent movements of the Western Isles ferries. Hunched over the equipment, the two second officers were rapt in concentration, the novelty of their task providing yet another unusual challenge.

Fingal's little inflatable boat, powered by outboard motor, boasted the luxury of wheel steering and a clear plastic screen for some elemental protection. It could work independently or complement the launches. Requiring lesser manpower for operation, its speed, small size, negligible

The inflatable, ready for action, in Sullom Voe, Shetland Islands. (Author's Collection)

draught, lightness and ability to resist expensive damage made it a valuable additional resource. With crew already on board, and with hands in a precautionary grip on the lifting hook, the boat was quickly hoisted overside from the main deck by crane.

Fingal's new-build replacement, *Pole Star (IV)*, does not have SOLAS lifeboats: her provision being that of liferafts. A rigid inflatable outboard-engined boat can act as a rescue boat. The ship is also provided with a single working craft for all boat operations. Of robust composite construction, which includes inflatable buoyancy chambers, she, too, proudly bears the name *Fingal* in celebration of her forebear.

CHAPTER 5

Skerryvore & Bell Rock Lighthouses

> It is one of the world's most beautifully engineered structures ... perhaps the
> most beautiful lighthouse in the world.

This is the informed opinion of R. Kinnear, a former principal civil engineer
of the Northern Lighthouse Board.

These superlative accolades refer to a Scottish rock lighthouse built on
a storm-swept reef a dozen miles into the Atlantic off the Inner Hebridean
isle of Tiree. Thanks to *Fingal,* her staunch wooden launch and experienced
coxswain, and the unusual official requirement to visit the rock with a
maintenance party, by standing on that very reef, utterly dwarfed by the
graceful might of the granite tower, these words rang true.

In the aftermath of an unseasonable storm, the Atlantic showed a benign
face, enabling a safe landing by boat amid the perilous rocky clefts and
shallows. The seamen and builders alike were sustaining a time-honoured
tradition; a direct link to earlier centuries and the era when creating such
towers – including Bell Rock on Scotland's east coast – ranked among the
greatest of human achievements.

June 2000: The unseasonal extreme bad weather of some 10 days earlier
had caused all sorts of disruption. For the NLB, at Skerryvore helipad,
contractors' building materials previously landed by helicopter from Pharos
were distributed from its rim position across the pad, rendering it unusable
by the helicopter.

In a period of subsequent calm, *Fingal's* launch landed a work party to
tidy up. There is an unwritten rule that it is often prudent to quit the rock
if attending by boat, not later than one hour after the start of the flooding

tide, even in good weather, and earlier if marginal. This, to avoid the possible swamping of the helipad by rogue swell waves that can build without warning, to sweep all before them off the pad, including a helicopter!

When manned, the inlet, known as the gully, was kept clear of kelp-weed by the Keepers. On this day, at near low water, an outer ladder was used – the heavily protected and stoutly-built boat yet encountering the surge and scuff of rasping rock to its long-suffering rubbing strakes.

The contractors had completed a steeple-jack's challenge, on a concave tower, to re-point the stone, and were to return to improve pathways and holding areas, away from the helipad. (Author's journal)

A week later, a return visit was made:

Fingal and a helicopter support team attended Skerryvore. The helicopter flew direct from the mainland. Several 'lifts' were moved elsewhere – including an over-height cement mixer – until the pilot was happy to land. (Author's journal)

At Skerryvore a shore party make good storm damage to repair materials previously dropped by helicopter from NLB ship *Pharos*. (Author's Collection)

Coxswain James Flett and crewman Lenny Brass carry out shuttle-work between *Fingal* and Skerryvore Lighthouse. (Author's Collection)

Bell Rock Relief

Captain Eric Smith provides the following description of a relief of the Bell Rock Lighthouse by boat.

When I joined the NLB in 1986, I was assigned to *Pole Star*, sister ship to *Fingal*. The Bell Rock was still manned at this time and the lightkeeper reliefs were carried out by boat. *Pole Star* was tasked to carry out a particular relief. The three keepers worked four weeks on and four weeks off with a relief every fortnight for either one or two keepers to swap. This ensured that the same three were not always on the rock at the same time and it also allowed for fortnightly storing. Although the rock had a helipad by then, the high water times, especially with the shorter days from autumn until spring, meant that daylight and relief day and low water would rarely coincide to allow regular reliefs by helicopter. It was therefore up to the ships to carry out reliefs.

Dependent on the weather, there were various options on relief day:
Full relief – when the keepers and all their gear and stores were landed at the grating;

Bare relief – when conditions were such that it was barely the keepers and their personal effects that were landed at the grating;

High water – effected on very quiet days when the launch was taken all the way in to the side of the tower at high tide;

Port Stevenson – using this named fairway to the north of the tower, but was only possible with a rubber dinghy and local knowledge.

The most common was using the main fairway approaching from the south. The time of relief was always three hours after high water at Leith. At this time, the water level at the grating was ideal for the launch to sit alongside for the required time. As it was on a falling tide, care had to be taken to carry out the relief in short order to avoid the boat being 'neaped'. The reason for not doing the relief during a rising tide was due to the risk of the launch being thrown onto the grating and getting damaged.

The first time I was involved with such a relief was shortly after joining the service. Due to tide times on that occasion, the relief was about 5.00 a.m. It was late autumn and dark, with a fair sea running. Always prior to relief time, we were in contact with the keepers on the rock to confirm that conditions were suitable for landing. After four weeks on Bell Rock, the conditions were always suitable! The end of the fairway was marked with a vertical steel bolt attached to a boulder. The top of the bolt had identifying retro-reflective tape, which the bowman in the boat illuminated with a torch or spotlight. The keeper on the rock stood at the end of the grating with a torch – this was both a signal to proceed and a mark to line up with the bolt for a safe route along the fairway.

Once alongside the grating, the relief was quickly completed: keepers and relief boxes on; keepers and gear off. The boat's crew then worked the launch astern around the end of the grating, using a line to hold her close. Once completed, it was full speed back down the fairway before the tide was away.

It was done very quickly, efficiently and skilfully by the boat's crew and there was a sense of satisfaction and a job well done by the time we got the keepers back on board the ship.

Dependent on the ship's programme, the keepers were landed by boat either at Granton or Arbroath.

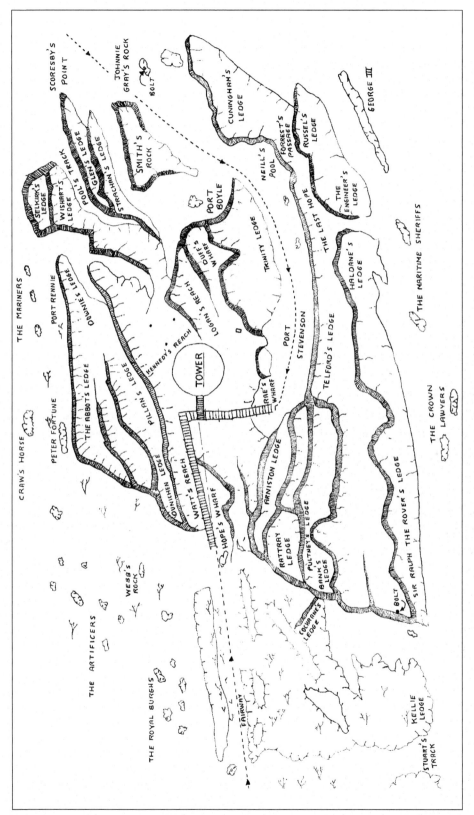

Hand-drawn chartlet to assist coxswains with boatwork at Bell Rock lighthouse. Original drawing by J. S. Galbraith: reproduced by Trevor Boult. (Author's Collection)

CHAPTER 6

On Close Inspection

Ports and harbours are legally required to provide and maintain appropriate local aids to navigation. These are charted, and listed in a particular Admiralty publication, which must be carried aboard ships. Every such local aid in Scottish waters is subject to annual inspection by the NLB, by whatever means appropriate, whether by visual observation from ship or by deployment of workboats for landing at remote jetties, etc. Such activity can bring interesting and amusing anecdotal incidents with officialdom and the public.

To many, the *Admiralty List of Lights and Fog Signals Volume A* may appear a dry and barely decipherable tome. Yet to mariners negotiating the coasts of the British Isles, it provides a wealth of information to supplement the precise and graphic detail colourfully depicted in esoteric symbols on modern navigational charts. Technology continues to replace the paper versions of traditional publications and charts with electronic equivalents – and brings with it both added advantages and hidden hazards.

Fingal's navigators were witness to the stealthy march of progress affecting the art and science of navigation, yet the landward hardware of physical structures endure in fundamental and reassuring form. Local references, such as the simplicity of two lit leading marks brought and kept in vertical alignment by a vessel's helmsman, give certainty of safe entrance into a tight harbour for a small-crew fishing boat, harassed by a strong tide; or a huge commercial ship keeping to mid-channel in an unhelpful cross-wind on departing an oil refinery complex.

At Sullom Voe, in Shetland, technology of an awesome scale is getting underway, as a fully laden supertanker makes ready to leave, fussed over by the powerful

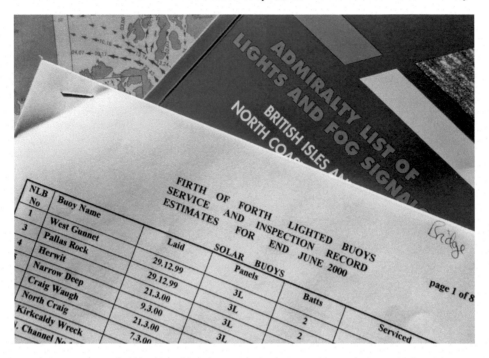

Service records and official publications used to carry out inspections of navigation aids. (Author's Collection)

and very necessary tugs in their livery of muted orange. The ship will use the very aids to navigation that *Fingal* is there to inspect; the channel buoyage, the 'minor' lighthouses on off-islets and headlands, with their tightly defined sectors of red, green, and white lights; the pairs of leading lights in their stubby towers, or atop their latticed floodlit pylons; or triangular marks strategically placed. Even to put the rudder over at the incorrect moment could potentially bring untimely disaster to such a ponderous leviathan. (Author's journal)

The Orkney Islands are an archipelago steeped in ancient archaeology of international acclaim. Their inhabitants, sometimes disparagingly referred to as 'farmers with boats', made their mark as the ablest of crews in the sailing ships of the whaling fleets. These watered at Stromness before heading into the wilds of the far north. Latterly, they embraced the oil terminal at Flotta and with it the accompanying maritime trappings that, like the Shetlands' Sullom Voe, brought huge vessels deep within its channels, where local knowledge is vital. Their volunteer lifeboat crews have performed numberless acts of heroism in the treacherous local waters of equal renown. Some paid the ultimate price.

Fingal carried out inspection duties in her erstwhile home waters with deference to the Orkneys' maritime heritage, to which she also contributed in sustained measure. She seemed to be as much of the navigational fabric as the ancient tower of St Magnus' Cathedral in the islands' capital of Kirkwall. The twelfth-century tower of Britain's most northerly cathedral – known as the 'Light in the North' – is strategically placed to act as a guide through a constriction in an approach channel.

On a February day, *Fingal* embarked on her work from her overnight anchorage in Inganess Bay, near Kirkwall:

> At the head of Inganess Bay is the airport. Given the snow and the gales, we had conjectured as to whether flights were being allowed. Weather had moderated, though there was still a good covering of snow.
>
> *Fingal* passed through the narrows – The String – guarded by Helliar Holm lighthouse. Balfour Castle on Shapinsay beyond. Boat inspection here, of harbour pier-head sector light (narrow white 'leading' sector, flanked by broad red, and green). Island ferry *Shapinsay* sailed. *Fingal* proceeded towards Skerry of Vasa. Daymark beacon inspected; landed by boat onto rocks. Ferry *Earl Thorfinn* passed via Vasa Sound, inbound for Kirkwall.
>
> *Fingal* proceeded towards Seal Skerry to inspect daymark beacon at southern approach to Eynhallow Sound. At mid-tide, rock was just awash. Not actually able to land. Lunch anchorage in Veantrow Bay, north Shapinsay.
>
> *Fingal* inspected many local marks by binoculars. Total for the day: 34 local authority marks throughout the Orkney north isles. Included inspecting the entrance channel buoyage and ferry pier-end lights at Stronsay Island. (Author's journal)

Inspection work may also be carried out direct from ship. The shore that bounds the southern limit of the Moray Firth is home to a concentration of traditional fishing communities, which are arrayed in linear parade along the northern county boundaries of Aberdeenshire, Banffshire, Moray and Nairn. Serrated by headlands and bays, there is navigable access to the elevated environs of the coast. On a bright and clear day, inspections can take an added pleasurable aspect, akin to a scenic excursion. As captain and chief officer took to the shoreward bridge-wing, armed each with a pair of binoculars, successive harbours were scanned for sight of the anticipated local marks. Meanwhile, the duty navigator was left to guide *Fingal* safely, sinuously within a passing distance, not closer than prudence, as they appeared.

Such occasions allowed for an almost intimate exploration of the coastline: individual houses, vehicles, a lone moped, people walking – pausing in their stride to see the unexpected apparition of *Fingal* sweep elegantly by. Local knowledge, too, was voiced: the night anchorage was at Pennan, which was hailed as the location for the film *Local Hero*; and,

Chief Officer John Ross cons *Fingal* through the Summer Isles on the approaches to Loch Broom and Ullapool. (Author's Collection)

Lying off the ferry terminal and harbour of Ullapool during inspections. (Author's Collection)

across Troup Head, Crovie is known for its houses being built so their gable ends face the sea.

The day's tally of harbours was recorded: MacDuff, Whitehills, Portsoy, Buckie, Lossiemouth, Hopeman, Burghead, Portmahomack.

At any location, the serendipity of timely chance can enhance inspections, whether scheduled or not. Just as it becomes second nature for a seafarer to cast a critical eye on life-saving equipment on board every time it is passed, navigation aids are almost absently scrutinised by those charged with their upkeep. Lying off the west-coast ferry terminal harbour of Ullapool, nestling in a sheltered alcove of Loch Broom, the quay frontage was visually patrolled with binoculars.

Further south, Loch Ryan has two ferry ports, Cairnryan and Stranraer, which connect to Northern Ireland. While attending inspections of Cairnryan, assistance was freely provided by the classic conventional ro-ro ferry *Stena Galloway* at her more-distant berth at Stranraer. The obliterating backdrop of the town's lights and the schedule of anticipated ferry movements precluded the checking of navigation aids in the long, narrow approach channel to the terminal. It was the Irish lilt of a familiar voice on the *Galloway* – the first ferry I historically cut my teeth on – that answered our radio request for sightings to be made, and which later confirmed all charted lights were operating correctly.

On a glorious spring day in 1999, as *Fingal* proceeded slowly outwards in the shallows of Inverness Firth after attending the shoal marker buoy at Middle Bank on the approaches to Kessock Bridge, the inflatable boat was sent away for a novel task. Unrestrained by the lack of water, the boat was free to roar at full speed and cover the miles out to the seaward entrance of the firth:

> ... to carry out an inspection of the slipway at Chanonry Point, for purposes of eventually landing a dignitary by boat later in the year. After the din of the 40-hp engine, all was quiet at the landing slip. Nearby, the stocky lighthouse tower was a dazzling white, sharing the guardianship of the entrance to the firth with mighty Fort George opposite. Rod-and-line fishermen looked on quizzically. A mature couple at the neat little car park offered discreet interest at the curious intrusion of this small boat out of nowhere, with the oilskin-clad figure intently making notes and taking photographs; the crewman patiently tending the boat. They asked: 'Is it far to the open sea?' 'No, just round that corner ... the Moray Firth!' (Author's journal)

This was my first use of a digital camera. On board ship, its images were processed onto computer and relayed by email to NLB headquarters

CHANONRY POINT SLIPWAY : INSPECTION

DAY: 19ᵀᴴ MAY 1999   TIME: ~1445 DST.   [1½ hours before HW SPRINGS at Inverness]

Inspection made by 'FINGAL's' inflatable boat.

The slipway consists of a substantial stone-jetty, and flanking wall to the "left-hand" side.   Both jetty and wall slope at a shallow angle into the sea. N.B. At the seaward end, the flanking wall makes a 90 degree angle. At the time of the visit, it was awash. The end is not marked.

The jetty ramp is of worn stone blocks, uneven underfoot. Up to half-tide level the ramp is covered in slimy green weed. Above this level it is clear of weed. Nature of the bottom appears to be mixed rock and shingle. The slope is similar to that of the jetty. It is shallow alongside. The z-boat could get to the jetty without the outboard grounding.

Disembarking would involve a downward step from a boat.

There are no useful mooring rings etc. visible.

Suggested landing times, based on HW Inverness :

Springs : approx 2 hours before, or equivalent ;
Neaps : approx 1 - 1½ hours before, or equivalent.

As observed :—

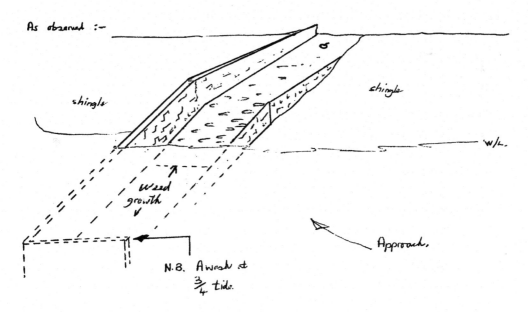

shingle   shingle
                                              w/L.
weed
growth
                                              Approach.
N.B. Awash at
 ¾ tide.

Photograph taken on digital camera.

Boult ⁵²/₀.

Report for submission to NLB by author, after inspecting the landing at Chanonry Point. (Author's Collection)

In advance of a visit by a dignitary to Chanonry Point at the entrance to Inverness Firth, the condition of the landing was inspected by *Fingal*. (Author's Collection)

in Edinburgh. These cameras were to become just one more piece of equipment to facilitate many aspects of maritime operations.

The East Neuk is a celebrated part of the Kingdom of Fife. Its south-facing shores flank the outer reaches of the Firth of Forth. Five separate and distinctive coastal settlements adorn this sun-blessed region: Elie, St Monans, Pittenweem, Anstruther and Crail. Each has their individual character and charm, but all are rooted in the sea. Their harbours are of historic interest and are prized subjects for artists and photographers alike. Pittenweem is home to the local fishing fleet. Neighbouring St Monans built many of these stout wooden craft at the famous yard of James Miller and slipped them for maintenance on the waterfront.

Fingal's inspection work once again unwittingly allowed the sharing of special local events. At St Monans:

Witnessed the launching of *Good Shepherd IV*, on a bright cheerful day, at James Miller's yard. This new steel-hulled vessel maintains the traditional name of the ferry link from Shetland to Fair Isle. Perhaps many of the observers are unaware that she will be hauled up on a special cradle at Fair Isle during stormy weather.

On the slipway, another acquaintance from my past: the Forth River Purification Board survey vessel, *Forth Ranger*. (Author's journal)

On a balmy summer day off the East Neuk of Fife, a beacon off Elie harbour was examined. (Author's Collection)

The Firth of Forth is a substantial sea area and contains a high concentration of navigation aids. The NLB provide major aids such as the lighthouses on the islands of May, Bass Rock and Fidra, and at Fife Ness. At the time of *Fingal's* inspections in 1999, it was noted:

> Local authority providers of navigation aids include: Forth Ports, British Gas, East of Scotland Water, Scottish Power, Scotrail, Royal Navy (Rosyth), Forth Road Bridge Engineering.
>
> Local authority buoyage inspections by boat at: Burntisland, Mortimer's Deep and its associated approach channels. Passage to Grangemouth Roads: inspections of beacons at Longannet Power Station, Bo'Ness, Bridgeness, Crombie Jetty, Charlestown, Rosyth, Port Edgar and Inverkeithing.
>
> At Port Edgar, brooded over by the bulk of the Forth Road Bridge immediately downstream, a stout white stubby tower encircled with day-glow orange marked Beamer Rock. In checking it:
>
> *Fingal* stemmed a considerable ebb tide and wind in mid-channel. All about was bustle; looming overhead the contrasting architectures of the bridges; road bridge traffic; trains on the rail bridge which was undergoing major refurbishment. At the top of its southern cantilever span, a proclamation of the number of days until the Year 2000. Auxiliary harbour craft plied; an inbound dredger for Rosyth cut north of Beamer Rock. (Author's journal)

The dredger was entering a commercial basin adjacent to the Royal Navy's facility at Rosyth. As with any military establishment, security is a major consideration. The NLB also had its duties here, and the navigation aids provided on site by the naval authorities were not exempted. Prior consent to carry out inspections had been received. A boat from *Fingal* was dispatched and it began work around the dock. Despite this, their activity drew interest from the Defence Police's own patrol craft, which set off in hot pursuit of the apparent infiltration by the boat and its shore party. As Donald, the inspecting officer, remarked to Harry the coxswain while negotiating a well-defended access to a navigation light: 'If they start shooting, don't wait for me!'

The boats themselves occasionally become casualties, such is the frequency and scope of their use. In the boisterous chop of a Shetland channel, the inflatable boat suffered a tear in the forward compartment. Becoming a graphic illustration of deflation, nevertheless the staunch little craft was towed back to ship by launch. Nothing daunted, the wet-through second officer continued his duties in the bigger boat.

Off the Fife shore, the long-suffering outboard engine succumbed to malfunction. On this occasion, the tow back to *Fingal* took on the jovial spirit of 'messing about in boats'. It was a thorny problem for the ship's engineers to rectify the mysterious fault in the engine.

Ship's boats occasionally suffer breakdown or operational damage. The inflatable was towed back to *Fingal*, in the Firth of Forth. (Author's Collection)

Unseen perils and heart-warming consequences can arise from inspection work:

> An afternoon of inspecting a miscellany of local authority marks, often unique constructions: for instance Leith Approach buoy – a glass-fibre catamaran float with spindly superstructure. To start the flashing sequence, a black bin-bag simulated darkness to trigger the sensor. Leith Sewage works, diffuser heads, marked by two cardinal buoys. (unlit)
>
> At Fisherrow harbour, checked the pier-end light, surmounting its angular tripod. Running in on a rising tide, with *Fingal* beyond sight in deeper water, the sandy beaches were admired, but with an eye to depth. Scrambling up the pier-end rungs, an expensive 'crack' in my pocket reduced a sentimental pair of sunglasses to ruin. An observer stood to watch our colourful and bizarre antics.
>
> During our visit to Fisherrow, our activities were noticed by an off-site local inhabitant who evidently thought we were of malicious intent and contacted the police: a mysterious launch appearing from seaward, as if some kind of raiding party to molest the light – doing odd things beneath the anonymity of a black bin-bag, then promptly vanishing from whence they came. In the course of enquiries the police contacted NLB headquarters next morning for clarification. (Author's journal)

Such public-spirited action was pleasing, as well as initially amusing. It was a quiet vindication of one routine aspect of the NLB's work, and an appreciation of the coastwise lights, which are given such close inspection.

CHAPTER 7

A Look at the Log

Extract from the author's diary:

VOYAGE '1': 21 JANUARY 1999 TO 18 FEBRUARY 1999

21st: 17.45: Join *Fingal* at NLB Depot, Stromness, in Mainland Orkney.

22nd: 09.00: Depart Stromness, destination anchorage in Broadford Bay, (SE Skye) Weather: SW-8, especially off Cape Wrath. [12-4 watch] 22.00: at anchor. Steamed 149 n. miles.

23rd: Weather unsuitable for buoy work. Remain at anchor in Broadford Bay.

24th: Attend 3 unlit buoys: **Gulnare Rock** (off NE Scalpay Island) **Penfold Rock** and **Jackal Rock**, in the Raasay Narrows. Passage north-about, via Sound of Raasay; inner route at Eilean Trodday, to anchorage in Ardmore Bay, at head of Dunvegan Bay, NW Skye. [12-4 watch] 17.00: at anchor. Steamed 57 n. miles.

25th: Attend unlit buoy **Bo Na Famachd** (off Dunvegan Castle) Passage to NLB Depot, Oban, via Sound of Mull. 18.00: arrived. Steamed 103 n. miles.

26th: 13.00: Depart, after loading new buoy for Avon Rock (Sound of Mull). Attend change-over of buoy at **Avon Rock**. Returned to Oban. Berthed alongside NLB tender *Pharos*. [12-4 watch] Steamed 25 n. miles.

27th: 09.00: Depart. Passage via Sound of Kerrera and Torran Rocks channel to Iona Sound. [9-12 watch] Anchored in Sound of Iona. Weather unsuitable for buoy work. Proceed to Colonsay for overnight anchorage, off Loch Staosnaig, by Salasaig. 17.30 arrival. Steamed 61 n. miles.

28th: 09.00: Depart. Return to Iona Sound. Attend **Iona Bank South buoy.** Anchor at lunch. Attend buoys at **Bo an Sliginach** and **Bogha Choilta.** Proceed to Oban. 18.00 arrival. Steamed 63 n. miles

29th: 09.00: Depart. Passage via Sound of Kerrera and Sound of Insh to attend Bono Rock buoy. Passage to anchorage near Lismore Lighthouse (east). Attend **Lady's Rock light,** to gauge acetylene bottle use, and inspect lantern. (by workboat: calm weather) Returned to Oban. 14.42 arrival. Steamed 30 n. miles. Loaded bunkers.

30th: 09.00: Depart. Attend **Ferry Rock SE,** and **Ardbhan Rock** buoys in Sound of Kerrera; also cardinal mark **Sgeir Rathaid North** in Oban Bay. Returned to NLB Pier. 12.00: arrival. Steamed 7 n. miles. ALL BUOYAGE WORK FOR 'YEAR 1998' COMPLETED.

31st: 08.00: Depart. Passage via Sound of Mull, Little Minch to overnight anchorage at Branahuie Bay near Stornoway. 18.00 arrival. Steamed 131 n. miles. [8-12 watch]

1st: 06.00: Depart. Proceed to Stromness: arrive 14.00. Land helicopter fuel, buoys ex-Oban, etc. 18.00: Depart for NLB-DGPS (satellite positioning system) trials [12-4 watch]. At midnight, steamed 185 n. miles. Passage north: west of Shetlands.

2nd: DGPS coverage trials at Position '1': 50 miles north of Muckle Flugga [SW 9-10 conditions]. Passage towards Position '2': 50 miles NW of Butt of Lewis. Steamed 204 n. miles. [12-4 watch]

3rd: DGPS coverage trials: 03.30: passed Schiehallion and Foinavon Oilfields. At Position '2' [SW 9-10 conditions]. Passage towards Aberdeen. Position at midnight: 4 miles SE of Duncansby Head. Steamed 272 n. miles.

4th: Arrive 09.42 at anchorage close east of entrance to Aberdeen Harbour. Relief by ship's boat of Captain Eric Smith and Chief Engineer Peter Wilson (proceeding on leave). Captain Alan Rore and Chief Officer John Ross join.

14.30: Depart anchorage. Coastal passage south to overnight anchorage in Montrose Bay (N) 17.00 arrival. Steamed 137 n. miles.

5th: 08.00: Depart, to complete DGPS coverage trials, east of Montrose. Passage to Aberdeen. Ship's boat to harbour to collect relieving Chief Engineer (previously storm-bound in the Orkneys). 14.30: Carry out leading light inspections at entrance to Aberdeen Harbour. Also sector light inspection of North Breakwater light, Peterhead. [8-12 watch] Night anchorage SSW of The Scares buoy (7 miles south of Peterhead) 17.45 arrival. Steamed 83 n. miles.

6th: 08.00: Depart. Passage north to Stromness. Enter Orkneys via Hoxa Sound and Scapa Flow. 17.30 arrival [8-12 watch] Steamed 112 n. miles.

7th/8th: At Stromness. Maintenance and repairs following storm-damage caused on February 2nd and 3rd.

9th: Repair work completed. 13.00: Depart via Scapa Flow, Sound of Hoxa, for passage to anchorage at Inganess Bay (near Kirkwall). 17.18 arrival. Steamed 49 n. miles.

10th: 08.30: Depart for inspections of local sea-marks (non-NLB) Included: **Balfour Harbour**, Shapinsay; **Skerry of Vasa beacon; Seal Skerry beacon.** Lunch anchorage at Veantrow Bay, North Shapinsay. Total for the day: 34 local authority marks throughout the north isles of Orkney. Also included approach channel buoyage, and 2 Fixed Green signal on ferry pier-head at Stronsay. Passage to anchorage at Backaskail Bay (South Sanday). 16.48 arrival. Steamed 43 n. miles.

11th: 08.30: Depart. Passage south to Pentland Firth. Midday anchorage at Gills Bay (Inner Sound). Boat inspection of **Stroma Skerries beacon**. Passage to Scapa Flow. Gauged **Scapa light-buoy** by boat. Passage to Stromness. 16.30 arrival. [8-12 watch] Steamed 76 n. miles.

12th: 08.30: Depart. Response to buoy casualty in Firth of Forth. Passage to night anchorage in St Andrews Bay. 23.18 arrival [8-12 watch] Steamed 183 n. miles. PS. Boat ashore at Aberdeen: Second Officer landed, to proceed on leave.

13th: 07.00: Depart. Passage into Firth of Forth. Attended RACON casualty at **Inchkeith Fairway buoy**. Local inspection of **Elie Ness beacon**. Inspected reported casualty to **Sand End buoy,** off Burntisland. 14.00: anchored off Granton. Boat to Granton, landing Second Engineer on leave. Collected delivery of engineering, GMDSS radios, and new RACON items. Passage to night anchorage in St Andrews Bay. 18.30 arrival. Steamed 95 n. miles.

14th: 08.30: Depart. Passage, with local authority light inspections at: **Johnshaven, Gordon, Stonehaven, Buchan Ness** and **Fraserburgh.** Night anchorage at Pennan Bay. 16.42 arrival. Steamed 98 n. miles.

15th: 08.30: Depart. Passage, with local authority light inspections at: **Macduff, Whitehills, Portsoy, Buckie, Lossiemouth, Hopeman, Burghead,** and **Portmahomack.** Night anchorage off Golspie (NW of Tarbat Ness). 15.48 arrival. Steamed 64 n. miles.

16th: 07.00: Depart. Passage to Stromness. 13.42 arrival. Steamed 78 n. miles.

17th: In-port working at Stromness.

18th: Crew proceed on leave.

CHAPTER 8

Mysteries of the 'Mechanical Garden'

In the Mercantile Marine, the navigating bridge of a ship is jokingly referred to as the 'Nervous Centre'. In similar vein, the machinery space is often celebrated as the 'Mechanical Garden': a mysterious realm upon which every facet of shipboard life depends.

Peter Wilson was Chief Engineer on *Fingal* during her final period of service with the NLB. He provides the following description of daily routines in the ship's engine room.

Engine room complement:

Chief Engineer; Second Engineer; Third Engineer; Engine Room Petty Officer/ Storekeeper; two Motormen.

Daily routine: vessel alongside at NLB depot:

06.00: Work commences. Prior to the galley equipment being turned on, the duty motorman changes from shore power to ship's power:-

Start the generator;

At the main switchboard, open the breaker from the shore to isolate from the ship's electrical distribution system;

Close the diesel generator breaker to provide electric power to the ship;

Close appropriate breakers, e.g. galley equipment, lighting, pumps, etc. Do so gradually to allow the generator to adjust to the load required;

Isolate the shore power from the pier and disconnect the cable from the ship and coil neatly.

The temporary power loss brings on the emergency lights which are then extinguished when power returns.

After breakfast, all departments commence day-work.

Second Engineer and night-duty Motorman exchange notes of observations, then decide what actions, if necessary, are to be taken. The Storekeeper will have checked all oil levels and consulted the Second Engineer. The Second and Third Engineers work on planned maintenance or in response to new requirements.

Chief Engineer attends to official paperwork: Engine Log Book entries at noon; scrutinise the information provided on engine- and machinery oil and water levels; fuel and oil consumption. If at the end of the month, transfer consumptions and remaining-on-board figures to abstracts, and general and reactive work effected. Examples of other routines include: consult with outside contractors; order spares and chase up outstanding orders. Consult with the Captain and Chief Officer in respect of the running of the ship and any maintenance of equipment in the Deck or Catering Departments. Address and monitor requirements of Health and Safety.

Preparing for sea:
Engine room prepared by Motormen:-

Main engines warmed through from either generator recirculation or the electric heaters;

Open valves from air receivers;

Start water and oil pumps. Oil pumps running at least one hour before engines on standby, to warm the internals of the engines.

In liaison with the navigator on watch, an engineer carries out all pre-sailing checks of critical and other systems as required between the Deck and Engineering Departments.

Respond to telegraph order from bridge to 'Stand-by'. One engineer operating port engine; one engine crew operating starboard engine. A further engine crewman attends the machinery space as an additional man. Both engines were manually operated and had to be attended to for starting, stopping and adjustment of speed. This required the telegraph to each engine being answered on each instruction from the bridge: for example if 'Half Ahead' was rung, the engine room confirms by ringing the response, then effecting the command by manual controls. Throughout all manoeuvres, whether in port, during buoy work, or on passage, oil and water temperatures had to be monitored and controlled.

Chief Engineer's roving duties during Standby:
To keep watch on:-

Latterly in *Fingal*'s life, movement of the bow was controlled by a 360-degree rotating variable speed azimuth thruster, driven by a Diesel Dorman engine;

Deck capstans and workboat davits, foredeck crane and deck buoy-maintenance equipment were operated by a common hydraulic system. The tank reservoir and pumps for the oil were located in the forward hold 'tween decks. This system required the Chief Engineer to be available to react quickly to any eventuality in the system.

Underway, there was the usual settling of the engine-room systems and machinery. Oil and diesel purifiers were on and their flow rates regulated.

On passage, the bridge would telegraph 'Full Away' which releases the engine room from 'Stand-by' status. Underway watch-keeping in the engine room would then commence. This was a manual process, requiring regular rounds of the machinery space.

Meal breaks and reliefs:

Under the then current rules and regulations, the Chief Engineer was not required to do a watch. It was a common courtesy to do evening-meal relief for the four-to-eight watch-keeper, and even to complete the watch. This was generally reflected also by the engine-room crew.

On a long passage, or an overnight steam, the Chief Engineer did the four-to-eight watch, in keeping with that of the Chief Officer. This made them available for contact with the outside world or anyone on the ship.

During 'smoko' and comfort visits, an engineer would provide cover as required.

During operations:

Particularly during buoy work, when the vessel necessarily would often be close to rocks, the engine room was on standby, with an additional man to respond to the effects of any grounding and puncture to the hull which, apart from the double bottom tanks, was single-skinned. An enclosed general service pump and a waterproofed electric motor powering it provided for such emergency. This could be used in conjunction with extended spindles operated from the plates above the main engines, level with the main switch board, to enable the opening and closing of valves to pump out the ingress of flood water. The engine room, shaft tunnel, workshop and stores were divided by a watertight bulkhead and associated door operated locally or remotely.

Night time alongside:

Hours of work were normally nine until four o'clock.

The crew shut the engine room down in the reverse order as previously described. The change from the steady low-decibel noise of the engines turned into a hissing when being stopped and the indicator valves being opened. This was to enable the engine to be turned to the correct position so as to start first time when required to do so. The cocks were closed after this.

From the gradual silence of the hissing to the silence of a shore-powered ship, where the loudest noise that could be heard was the lapping of the sea through an open porthole, or someone turning the page of their newspaper. Then again – there was always a 'leaky tap…'!

Magnetic Personality:

During the Second World War many ships were fitted with degaussing gear as a countermeasure against magnetic mines. As a precaution, some vessels were installed with this equipment until the late 1960s. *Fingal* was one such. The installed degaussing system rendered the ship's own magnetism neutral to the sensors incorporated in mines and was achieved by altering the electric current in the ship's coils. After every refit during the early life of *Fingal*, when on sea trial, the degaussing system was recalibrated.

Second Engineer Bob Hutton at the main electrical switchboard. (Author's Collection)

Second Engineer Colm O'Brien and Chief Engineer Peter Wilson diagnose a faulty outboard motor. (Author's Collection)

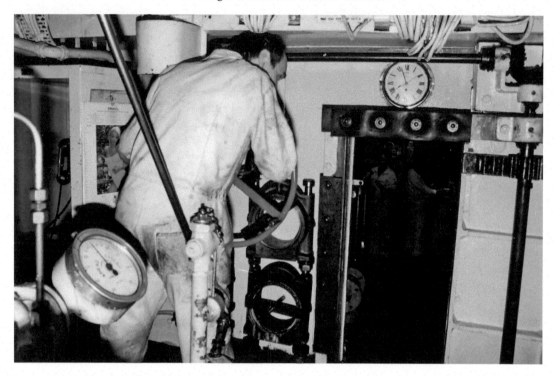

Testing the local controls of the watertight door that divided the machinery spaces. (Author's Collection)

The engineer officers effect a repair to the deck crane's hydraulics. (Author's Collection)

CHAPTER 9

NLB Depots & In-Port Work

The NLB tenders represent the principal seagoing resource to facilitate the delivery of its obligations for the safety of navigation. They are necessarily supported by many vital shore services, which include official depots. Latterly in the career of *Fingal*, these were at Oban, and Stromness in Orkney, where *Fingal* was ultimately based. Following substantial upgrading, Oban is now the sole depot.

The NLB ships also regularly call at out-ports throughout Scotland where the use of in-house and contracted road vehicles offers logistical support away from the depots, and where periodic maintenance of the ships' fabric can be carried out.

A depot provides comprehensive services to the ships, including: all-tide berths with additional bad-weather mooring capability; facilities to enable taking stores, fresh water, fuel bunkers and other oils; and garbage and waste oils removal. Spacious and fully equipped workshops allow for full refurbishment or repair of all types of buoyage, and a stock of components is maintained for these and all other navigation aids. As helicopters are integral to the maintenance of lighthouses, depot facilities also cater for their operations.

Oban depot provides ready walking access to the amenities of the town. A route to a large supermarket embraces the usual discreet 'hole in the fence' that is a hallmark of seafarers the world over. It was a common sight on the first evening after an arrival at Oban for crew to be seen returning with supermarket bags bulging with personal victuals to boost provisions: fruit, quality butter, jars of honey …

A renowned resort, Oban – the 'Little Bay' – fringes a near-perfect horseshoe-shaped harbour. Its historic North Pier and wide frontage of the ferry terminal are complemented equally by the Lighthouse Pier, and its goings-on are much observed by sea-food-eating tourists strolling along the waterfront. Of an evening, they could also be joined by off-duty individuals from *Fingal*. For some, Oban is home. Others might take to the heights of McCaig's Folly for a grand view to the west, or promenade to Dunollie Light at the northern entrance to the bay, delighting in an illicit bag of chips.

In Orkney, Stromness was also home for crew. For others, with a bent to romanticism and whose homes were far-distant, it is another adopted home-from-home. Its own facilities, by-ways and scenic paths fall to be explored after the day's work was done.

In mid-July, the town hosted a much-anticipated gathering:

Fingal arrived at Stromness at 6.00 p.m.; coincidentally at the start of 'Shopping Week'. The Daft Raft Race from Ness slipway was just beginning. In the main street: coloured lights and bunting, shop windows dressed fancily, the skirl of pipe bands, foreign tongues, people thronging. There was extra Post Office trade, but the black cat on the counter was aloof and unimpressed. Events went on throughout the week, including a grand parade and firework display. *Fingal* and the ferry *St Ola* dressed with flags. Rescue services displayed in the harbour: the Coastguard Sea King helicopter, the lifeboat, a dive-boat 'in distress', a liferaft and a 'man overboard'. (Author's journal)

At Stromness, keeping *Fingal's* decks snow-free and shipshape for work in port. (Author's Collection)

A pleasant summer day in Orkney. (Author's Collection)

Buoy maintenance by shore staff at Stromness depot. (Author's Collection)

Loading refurbished buoys.
(Author's Collection)

A subsequent late-afternoon arrival found the off-duty watchman and engine-room storekeeper poised at the gangway; one shouldering a golf bag of clubs, the other with a wheeled trolley. They set off with enthusiasm for eighteen holes on the spectacularly sited local golf course.

The golf club also hosted a special wedding reception for the daughter of a deceased seaman of *Pole Star*. His widow asked Captain Smith if the wedding in Stromness might be enhanced through their historical associations with the NLB, given that it was not actually possible for the ceremony to take place on *Fingal*. Captain Smith recalls: 'I was quite happy to record in the Official Log Book the fact that Linda, daughter of Ronnie, had got married on that day in Stromness, and duly signed it myself.' It was a pleasure for me to be a small part in this kindness, by witnessing the captain's signature with my own in the official document.

Workboat maintenance alongside at Invergordon, Cromarty Firth. (Author's Collection)

As most of *Fingal's* work was labour-intensive and carried out in daylight hours, the ship generally went to an appropriate overnight anchorage in the vicinity, or alongside at a courtesy berth provided by the nearest harbour or port: Lerwick, Stornoway, Mallaig, Invergordon, Dundee, Leith.

Being in port allowed for the proper respite of deck and engineering departments from the state of readiness of a vessel at anchor. It enabled brief 'R-n-R' – rest and recuperation – ashore, and the ability to maintain the ship, especially overside or where an unmoving platform was desirable, such as in exposed and elevated work.

Near the top of the tall foremast, following storm damage, the navigation light needed attention. Without foot-rungs, access was by the traditional means of Bosun's chair hoisted aloft. In Invergordon, a spell of idyllic summer weather, and the replenishment of the fresh water tanks, enabled high-pressure hosing to wash down the salt-encrusted hull and upperworks – the scars of yet another boisterous and sea-drenching earlier passage. A workboat was swung outboard on its davits for easy maintenance from the quayside.

Advantage could also be taken for opportunistic storing, whether for the ship, or an individual's home:

> Leith; Drive with Ian, Chief Steward, in his own car to Bookers cash-and-carry on the outskirts of Musselburgh, armed with shopping list for Ned, the Cook: catering boxes of teabags, bags of pre-cut chips, flour, salad vegetables: a good deal in 'bulk' mayonnaise. (Author's journal)

In Stornoway, a native of the island of Lewis was quick to make the most of a scheduled but infrequent visit to his doorstep. Donald returned by car to the ship with his young son. All manner of shrewd bargain purchases made the previous evening in Oban were offloaded: pride of place, a set of aluminium stepladders.

CHAPTER 10

Toils for Oil

Until the 1960s, all UK oil supplies were imported, at great expense. The discovery of North Sea oil in the late 1960s initiated what has been described as 'one of the major industrial achievements of the twentieth century'.

Today, along the central spine of the North Sea, a huge number of complex and alien-looking structures support this industry, which has been so vital to the UK. The largest of these are moveable exploration rigs and fixed production platforms. As technologies progressed, these installations have been joined by massive moored floating facilities.

As exploration continues in Scottish waters, new fields have come into production in other areas, notably inshore in the Moray Firth, and to the west of the Shetlands.

All such sensitive installations are prey to the potential dangers of collision from passing shipping. In response, they are required to provide statutory aids to navigation, in the form of special lights and fog signals. These are subject to annual inspection by the appropriate Lighthouse Authority, acting on behalf of what is now the Department of Energy & Climate Change. The area covered by the NLB extends from west of the Shetlands, and from east of the Shetlands to the English border. *Pole Star* was regularly assigned this task of inspection until it was sold in 1993, after which *Fingal* took over the duty.

The work is generally carried out between November and January to take advantage of the long hours of darkness. However, it is also a period of potentially severe weather. *Fingal's* sea-keeping qualities enabled this arduous task to be carried out over a protracted period where ship's staff doubled up on extended watches. They were joined by senior members of the shore establishment who carried out the observations, checks, and records. It is not unknown for the inspection to span two weeks, if shelter needs to be sought, or if the vessel slowed considerably on passage to make conditions sustainable and maintain safe headway.

Fingal's final 'Inspection of Offshore Structures' took place in November 1999. It officially started from her overnight anchorage in St Andrews Bay, off the Fife shore. Two inspecting officers from headquarters had boarded, one of which was Captain Jack Ross, a former master of *Fingal*. The voyage spanned six days and the distance steamed was logged as 1,533 nautical miles, terminating at the depot in Orkney.

On the initial passage east, in anticipation of potential prolonged exposure to adverse conditions, all mooring ropes were stowed below decks. The securing devices of the lifeboats and launches in their davits were tightened further, the decks generally cleared and weathertight openings battened down. The cargo derricks, normally kept 'topped', were lowered until horizontal in their securing crutches. The moveable contents of cabins, galley and workshops also benefitted from close scrutiny.

It is unusual for any NLB ship to visit locations with an east longitude. The inspection voyage found *Fingal's* North Sea charts essentially being given their annual airing: charts which, together with all her sizeable folios of charts, were meticulously kept up-to-date by the navigators, enabled by the issue of weekly Notices to Mariners supplied by the Admiralty.

Prior to the inspection, all operating companies were given warning by NLB Operations and issued with particulars of every navigation aid to be checked at each location. The first installation inspected was Norpipe, an unmanned structure designated A/S 37-4-A that lies on the Ekofisk to Teesside oil pipeline. Arriving in the early evening darkness, and keeping beyond the 500-metre safety zone that circles all such structures, we verified the statutory lights, which, in this case, comprised two white and two red lights flashing together the Morse letter 'U' (..-). Passing downwind of the installation until the activated fog signal was audible, its phase was timed with a stopwatch. The illumination and visibility of any identifying name board was also checked.

For the duration of the voyage, due to the added workload, bridge watches around the clock comprised alternating six-hour periods of duty, fulfilled by the Captain and Junior Second Officer, rotating with the Chief Officer and Senior Second Officer. It was a period of quiet rebellion, where the customary wearing of uniform was displaced by more casual attire and the growing shadow of stubble on chins: bad weather and an incessant, lively and tiring motion had indeed arrived!

Captain Jack Ross,
Inspecting Officer,
checking the audibility
and timing of the fog
signal at Curlew oilfield.
(Author's Collection)

Relieved at midnight for a nominal six hours off duty, when 6.00 a.m. came the droll greeting was merely, 'it's as if we've never been away!' In the southerly gale, running north with the engines stopped, *Fingal* made sedate progress conveniently towards Banff oilfield.

Overnight at the Fife oilfield, the ship was close to the boundary with the Norwegian sector. We shared the same sea space with the safety standby vessel *Tiree*. The crews of such vessels must endure the worst of weathers in keeping station to act as a quick-acting lifeline in emergencies to the offshore communities that populate the oil and gas platforms beyond the horizon. Later, on a chart, next to Piper Bravo, was the poignant symbol 'Piper Alpha Wreck': an historic testament and reminder of the real price of oil. For company, these dedicated standby vessels witness the comings and goings of supply ships, helicopters and occasional 'seismic' survey ships, while fending off fishing and passing commercial vessels that may appear to be straying too close to their valuable charges.

In a change from *Fingal's* routine, there was a stark contrast between attending diminutive buoys in the remote convoluted channels of some West Coast defile amid the grandest of natural scenery and the high-tech of Rig World, with its orange and neon-lit cities on stilts, and alien flaring of burnt-off gas. The radar screen gave the impression of having contracted a rash; such was the density of the surrounding structures.

With customary resignation, the stormy seas were stoically accepted. In the cabin, the chair was laid on its back and drawers were held shut with paper wedges. The door curtains pendulumed rhythmically along the length of alleyway. In the galley, the cook worked miracles, producing pastries, rolls, light sponges and main dishes. In extremes, there were bacon sandwiches for breakfast. The manifold discomforts in the engine room were alleviated by crossing off the names of the unseen rigs, as a desperate mark of progress.

In a lull, the carpenter took to the foredeck to sound the freshwater tanks, harden up the wooden wedges around the sides of the tarpaulined hatch and sledgehammer the ports to swing and allow shipped water to cascade freely over the side. On the fo'c'sle, the security of the anchors and watertightness of the lockers that held the anchor chains were checked. He returned, satisfied.

By the following day, the wind had returned, this time from the north, bringing with it head seas with which to grapple. Engines now ran at half ahead, laboriously maintaining the same northerly progress so easily made the previous day. Helmsmen each took half-hour tricks at the wheel to keep the heading. The watchmen were glad to stay out of their cabins, as a change from the movement and claustrophobia of below, where the lack of television or radio was felt. Sighting the brass engine telegraphs exposed on the open bridge-wings, there were resigned sighs at seeing them tarnished. They were generally a source of pride, lovingly maintained to a high-reflecting polish. Extra elbow grease would eventually be needed to restore them.

The inspections continued throughout. The northernmost limit was the BP Magnus oilfield, 100 miles northeast of the Shetlands. The voyage concluded at the three well-spaced installations of the Beatrice oilfield lying off the Caithness coast.

A total of 110 installations were inspected. Faults or inadequacies to the navigation aids were initially relayed by radio from *Fingal* to the primary installation, and followed up officially from the NLB in Edinburgh.

Reverting to the normal three-watch system of four hours' duration came as a luxury for the passage back to Stromness, via a brief overnight anchorage in the welcome stillness of Scapa Flow. However, normality was not to last long, as preparations for another necessary periodic event – drydocking – got underway.

CHAPTER 11

Destination Drydock

All ships operating around the globe are subject to regulations designed to ensure that they are maintained in a seaworthy condition and to keep their fabric and equipment in good order. These regulations are both national and international. To comply, it is often a periodic necessity for a ship to be put in drydock, so as to access areas that otherwise would be beyond reach, followed by a lay-up period after re-floating. It can herald a huge sea change in the life of the ship, her crew and shore staff. *Fingal's* final drydocking as an NLB tender took place on Tyneside in north-east England, towards the end of 1999.

There are two main regulatory organisations: the Flag State, and the Classification Society. For *Fingal*, Flag State control was the Maritime and Coastguard Agency (MCGA). The Classification Society was Lloyd's Register, which took care of most surveys on behalf of the MCGA. However, some surveys, such as that for safety equipment, are carried out by the MCGA.

Ships are grouped into several classes, depending on their type: passenger vessels, cargo vessels, tugs, etc. *Fingal* was a 'Class 7' ship and her certificate of class denoted which regulations and surveys applied.

The NLB's shore-based technical superintendent pools together all the survey and specific work requirements to produce a drydock specification – the 'spec'. Throughout the preceding months, *Fingal's* Captain, Chief Engineer and Chief Officer will have submitted wish lists of jobs they would like to have done during the docking. All this information forms the basis for the tender, which is submitted to suitable ship-repair yards. Some of the work will be carried out by the yard, while others will be to the order of a specialist contractor.

The major work done in drydock is to the underwater hull and fittings. The hull will be water-washed and the paint coatings inspected, with any suspect areas being sandblasted or disked prior to new coatings being applied. The whole underwater hull will be painted with antifouling paint, which inhibits marine growth, and top coat on the areas above water.

Typical items of work include overhaul of cranes, deck machinery, winches and anchor windlasses, fresh water tanks, engines and bridge equipment, fridges and sanitary systems, and any work necessary on sea valves or to the propellers, shafts and rudders. On completion, Flag State and Class surveyors inspect the vessel. If satisfied, certificates are issued or endorsed for a further specified period.

'Shipshape and Bristol fashion' is just one of many commonly used but only partially understood maritime expressions. The orderliness of a well-run ship in her usual sea-going capacity is drastically compromised when in drydock. Literally out of her element, a ship becomes landlocked and stranded, gradually taking on the attributes of a building site, or even one of demolition. Those in the know, who stand by a ship in drydock, and who are familiar with her earlier good looks, can still be prey to doubts that she'll ever be the same again. Yet always the miracle happens. Dealing with drydocking is very much an attitude of mind: ignoring the mess and mayhem, the noise and grime; to engage instead with the expression, 'you can't make an omelette without first breaking eggs'.

For *Fingal*, the physical process that would see her transformed temporarily into a building site began at Stromness. All superfluous equipment and stores were landed to the depot. On departure for the southerly passage towards the Tyne, as *Fingal* swung off the berth, Captain Rore remarked on the bridge-wing with resignation: 'The ship always seems to look her smartest when going to drydock'.

Methodically, the carpenter moved throughout the accommodation, unscrewing and labelling brass clocks, barometers and other shiny items of potential 'souvenir' value for any opportunistic light fingers that might be passing while in dock. From portholes, bunks and cabin-door entrances, the decorative curtains were also removed prior to being sent ashore for cleaning. Sheets of cloth were issued to protect the carpets. The homeliness of cabins had been replaced by stark practicality, with only discreet family pictures above the desk remaining for the time being. The wooden-decked alleyways were protected with heavy-duty brown paper, secured with broad tape. It would not take long for the shuffling tread of many grimy boots to remove the shine.

Fingal followed her usual dramatically scenic route south across Scapa Flow, through Hoxa Sound and issuing into the Pentland Firth, after passing the island of Swona for an open-sea passage across the broad maw of the Moray Firth. Rounding the busy corner off Rattray Head, between Fraserburgh and Peterhead, the day's run was concluded in the roads off Montrose for overnight anchorage. Although bound for drydock, *Fingal* was still capable of carrying out her primary duties:

> 10th: 08.30: Depart. Attend Montrose approach buoys at Annat Shoal, and Scurdie Rocks. Passage to Firth of Forth. Night anchorage off Inchkeith.

> 11th: 08.30: Depart. Attend buoy casualties at Pallas Rock, West Gunnet, North Channel No. 6. Passage to Tyneside. 19.18: Arrive night anchorage in Tyne Roads. (Author's journal)

The preceding passage from the Firth of Forth was another satisfying coastal transit, passing the great sentinel of Bass Rock in its wintry solitude, devoid of the teeming thousands of gannets that surround, occupy and whiten its lofty bulk throughout the breeding season. These local waters are the precursor of the southern limits of Scottish waters on the east coast and which were latterly visited infrequently by *Fingal*. The major tower lighthouse at Barns Ness near Dunbar, and the waypoint lighthouse perched dramatically on the spectacular cliffs of St Abb's Head, are the last principal lights before English waters – and the jurisdiction of Trinity House – are entered. They are dramatically represented off the Northumberland coast by the Longstone Lighthouse, guardian of the seaward expanse of low islands that make up the Farnes. It is also celebrated as the erstwhile home of the life-saving heroine, Grace Darling.

On the day *Fingal* passed, daylight had waned and the blink of Longstone flashed welcomingly in proper sequence, the seconds of its rhythmic phased signal automatically counted by the watchkeeper – as if keeping a friendly or critical eye on the workings of the NLB's sister organisation 'south of the border'!

It was the substantial local authority lights at the ends of the two mighty granite piers defining the entrance to the River Tyne that marked time for *Fingal* at anchor to the north of them. The ship was rocked gently by a ground swell and there was much domestic activity in cabins during the evening, as bags were being packed early with belongings. They would soon be offloaded to a variety of shore accommodations while *Fingal* was in dock. I found myself finalising the accounts for crew telephone bills and filling brown pay packets with wads of cash towards crew subsistence ashore.

The following morning, the first hint of twilight offered promise of a later poetic grey dawn breaking. Outward bound from North Shields, fishing boats cast long reflections of their steaming lights on oily smooth and inky water. *Fingal* was all prepared and, on the darkened bridge, pairs of eyes wandered frequently towards the harbour entrance, anticipating the appearance of the pilot launch and its giveaway identifying lights of 'white-over-red': a signal easily recalled by the less-than-flattering saying, 'White hat: red face'.

The launch *Bewick* duly arrived alongside. The pilot and launchman scrutinised the boarding ladder. In unmistakable and welcome Geordie brogue, the good-humoured pilot happily observed, 'It's only a short one'. Rigged at a bulwark on the low working deck, there was barely any climbing for the pilot, who then stopped to admire the carpenter's fine handiwork of the portable inboard steps, which conveyed him with some style down from the bulwark top to deck level.

With introductions on the bridge and a necessary exchange of information about the ship, the plan for the up-river passage and entry into the drydock was inevitably conducted with mugs of steaming brews in hand, as *Fingal* squared up to pass between the piers.

Professional familiarity with major harbours throughout Scotland is a satisfying by-product of working for the NLB. These, and lesser harbours, also had personal associations for many of *Fingal's* crew as their home ports. Tyneside was an outlier, almost a foreign destination, bringing with it the novelty of fresh experience. To me, however, Tyneside was home and I relished this occasion of homecoming.

The broad expanse of estuary, which opens out between the piers, was stamping ground for racing sailing dinghies when a youth; the wreck buoys and channel buoys, unofficially requisitioned as course markers, belonged to a lateral system now long defunct. A fine promenade on the north shore replaced high, crumbling cliffs, from which vantage the fate of the notorious wreck of *Oregis* on the Black Midden rocks left a deep early impression of the unforgiving power of sea and storm.

North Shields fish quay, a shadow of its former self, held memories of lobster potting and teenage initiation of gutting huge live cod on the heaving deck of a trawler fishing on Dogger Bank. The twin white towers of leading marks remain as daylight guides through the piers, but their lights are gone and their notations struck off navigational charts. At the RNLI, a new Severn-class lifeboat had but recently taken up station.

On the south bank, the much-enlarged sea school of the nautical college recalled the mysteries of wire splicing, rigging Bosuns' chairs, taking heavy rowing gigs onto the river in winter to get chill-blains and blistered hands, the discipline of lecturers trying to instil principles of navigation and ship construction to weekend-weary cadets.

On the first great bend, where Trinity House lightvessels historically drydocked, a complex of opulent flats and penthouse apartments trumpeted modern trends, which were taking over both sides of the river. Previously, ship-repair yards, bustling quays, dusty coal staithes and fleets of tugs at mooring buoys defined the lower reaches of the Tyne.

Two more reaches of the river were negotiated before approaching the environs of the drydocks and their attendant cranes. The pilot intimated, 'We're just going in next to *Isle of Lewis*.' This relatively new Cal-Mac ro-ro ferry served the busy Scottish route across the Minch between mainland Ullapool and the Outer Hebrides. As a Stornoway man, Donald, *Fingal's* Senior Second Officer, made a jokingly disparaging remark about the ship he regularly travelled on and which became a stalwart of the crossing for a further fifteen years.

There is both art and science in successfully placing a ship in drydock. Physical aspects involve manoeuvring into a tight space, holding in a precise position until the fluid process of emptying the dock and converting a heavy floating object into a wholly land-supported structure is played out in slow motion. The mathematics of ships' stability would have been carefully considered and applied before *Fingal* had even departed for the voyage south. Arrival draughts fore and aft were agreed between ship and dock, as were dispositions of bulk liquids in the various fuel, ballast and fresh water tanks. Calculations concerning stability at critical times during the draining of the dock were computed and set on record. A textbook dryly offers explanation:

> When entering a drydock, a vessel should be trimmed slightly by the stern, as the stern-frame structure has the strength to withstand the stress imposed and the trim aids positioning of the vessel on the keel blocks. The vessel should have adequate initial stability to withstand the losses sustained during docking. Once in the dock, the stern is positioned and the water pumped out until the sternpost takes the blocks. From this time, the vessel is not free floating, yet cannot be supported externally, as the water level continues to fall, the buoyancy upthrust reduces and is replaced by an upthrust through the sternpost from the blocks.
>
> The period between taking the keel blocks aft and taking the blocks along the vessel's length is the 'critical period'. During this period, the vessel is changing her trim from that on entering to the trim of the blocks. This change of trim is caused by the force of the upthrust through the stern-frame. A similar critical period is experienced during undocking, from the time of leaving the blocks forward until the vessel floats free. It is important that a careful note be made of the position of all weights and tank soundings, so

that the vessel can be returned to the same condition as when she entered the dock.

Arriving at a time when tidal stream and river current across the dock threshold were minimal, *Fingal* landed her shoulder gently on the entrance knuckle. Headline ropes were sent ashore and turned onto the barrels of the windlass. They were used to control and check the movement of the bow, initially in squaring up, and thereafter to hold the ship central in the dock. Likewise, when the stern ropes could be rigged they acted similarly at the rear.

Hidden beneath *Fingal*, on the dock bottom the preparatory efforts of the repair yard remained as yet invisible. Along the central spine of the dock was ranged a close set of keel blocks, subtly adjusted in position to the particular requirements of the ship. These were augmented by side blocks, more widely disposed yet as accurately placed, to match up with strength members on the hull and, as importantly, to avoid locations needing access, or areas of vulnerability.

Completely in the dock, the sea-gate was closed. In the settled water, adjustments to *Fingal*'s position were made by careful use of the ship's ropes and, at bow and stern, by two pairs of hand-cranked wire purchases, which could make small sideways movements of the hull. At each end of the dock, the exact centreline was marked by a water-filled bucket, into which hung a dampened plumb-line. Monitored by a dock official who hand-signalled to work colleagues at the purchases, *Fingal*'s lateral position was maintained as the dock water drained.

Careful observation of the draught marks at the stern was the only way to determine when the ship finally started taking to the blocks; such was the subtlety of this important moment. As *Fingal* began apparently to rise from the grimy water, with her measurement of depth at the stern decreasing, her trim also began to alter. Almost imperceptibly, the bow began to lower until, landed fully along her length, the remaining draught marks at the bow began to appear. As the last of the water was pumped clear, only a gentle cascade at the side of the sea-gate trickled in from the river and dissipated via a sump.

In her state of transition, there was an unnatural silence on board as machinery stopped. *Fingal*'s lights went out, save for emergency illumination, as shore electrical power was instated. A fire main was connected to a hydrant and other ancillary services addressed. In the galley, the huge cooking range, on throughout the year, began to cool slowly to a cold, lifeless slab.

The ship surrendered her customary self-sufficiency with good grace. At the bow, the carpenter removed the bell for safe-keeping. In advance

Docking adjacent to the CalMac Western Isles ferry *Isle of Lewis*. (Author's Collection)

Fingal squarely on the blocks ... (Author's
Collection)

... dwarfed by the dockyard cranes.
(Author's Collection)

of the substantial gangways being rigged, officers were craned to the dockside to attend the first formal meeting between ship's staff, the board superintendent and dock officials.

Increasingly distressed boiler suits, work boots and layers of warm clothing became normal attire, as much for wearing inside the now winter-cold ship as for making the long and steep-stepped trek to the dock bottom, or to the less-than-fragrant facilities provided and shared ashore.

Day one had been a long day. At its close, the standby crew dispersed variously for the night to a variety of accommodations: hotels, a self-catering flat on the seafront at Cullercoats. Or home: I was lucky!

Succeeding days passed to the many and changing requirements of the dockyard work schedule, aided in advisory capacity by ship's staff who otherwise occupied a monitoring role. There was, at least, little recourse to the wearing of waterproofs, with days of cold, crisp clarity, although surprisingly colourful under the sun's fleeting midday brightness.

The incumbent standby crew attended *Fingal* for six days before coming to the end of their four-week rota, handing over to the other shift, which completed the remainder of the drydocking. Journeys home for most were more lengthy than usual. It was a convenient change for me. I only needed a brief transit on the Tyneside Metro from Wallsend to Tynemouth.

On our next meeting, *Fingal* would once again be in full operation, generally as smart and shipshape as before, and with any glitches that are a normal part of post-drydocking resolved.

A work in progress. (Author's Collection)

A work in progress. (Author's Collection)

CHAPTER 12

A Testing Trial

Today, the term GPS – Global Positioning System – is in common and casual circulation around the world by the public. This space-based satellite navigation system was created and maintained by the United States government, and is made freely accessible to anyone with a suitable receiver. Advances in technology and miniaturisation have now made it available to any ordinary individual in the street. The system provides critical capabilities to military, civil and commercial users around the world. Its maritime applications are well established.

Early GPS accuracy was in the order of about 100 metres. The NLB developed differential corrections using some of its own lighthouses as base correction stations, which improved accuracy to about 10 metres. During the first Gulf War, the Americans enhanced the system accuracy to less than 5 metres, but the earlier 'error' was restored after the war.

Commercial shipping now uses GPS information as an input into a range of navigational equipment, and small devices are commonplace even in small private yachts. As their use – and reliance upon them increases – so, too, does the need for the level of accuracy to be enhanced and reliably maintained. The NLB has responsibility for the provision of DGPS – Differential GPS – in Scottish waters.

Three NLB lighthouses were equipped in their modified role as base correction stations, spaced to give proper coverage throughout the required sea areas. These are: Sumburgh Head, at the southern tip of the Shetlands; Butt of Lewis, at the northern extremity of the Outer Hebrides; and Girdle Ness, by Aberdeen. Following their completion, in-house trials needed to be carried out in working sea conditions to verify coverage and provide feedback on any weaknesses found. *Fingal* was tasked to test the system.

Three prime geographical locations were assigned for *Fingal* to monitor the signals: 50 miles north of Muckle Flugga, north of the Shetlands; 50 miles north-west of the Butt of Lewis; and east of Montrose in the North Sea. The work was carried out in early February, a period of very real and wintry weather in exposed locations:

> DGPS coverage trials, in south-west storm force 10 conditions. Beyond the bridge windows, elemental forces raged. Engines; one on half ahead, the other on full manoeuvring revs. Violent motion: pitch, yaw, roll, plunge, and rear. Ahead, the low sun was blinding. On the fo'c'sle, the ship's bell clanged gently from the motion. Inside the bridge, wind-forced spray drove through the top of the wooden weather door, to cascade … Yet, those on duty on the bridge calmly monitored the equipment and logged the information. (Author's journal)

Each of the three trial stations was switched off for several hours. The quality of daytime signal coverage and any overlap of other stations were monitored at the prime locations. A passing comparison was made about the relative comfort of differently sized vessels in commonly shared sea conditions:

> On passage to prime station 2, deviate to pass south of the Schiehallion and Foinaven oilfields. The various rig lights on the horizon were sighted at 20 miles. Fingal was to carry out annual inspections of these rigs, but weather conditions and lack of time precluded this. On station in among the rigs, the FPSO – Floating Production, Storage and Offloading vessel – was also lit up, looking almost like a huge cruise ship; head to sea, her restrained and very slow pitching motion emphasizing her vast size. Towards her bow, the great lattice tower held at its peak a great flare-off of flame. Held securely against the worst of conditions by a splayed array of many anchors, her long pipe attached to the seabed well-heads by long flexible risers. Unlike *Fingal*, a free spirit and a seemingly insignificant vessel carrying only navigation lights, this was a futuristic and technological metropolis that made so light of the sea's tumult. Conditions that inspire the envious and derisory remark: 'they're probably playing snooker on the bridge … !' (Author's journal)

CHAPTER 13

The Millennium

In the days before an aircraft had broken through the sound barrier, the scientific world was troubled as to what effects might result. Fifteen years before the close of the twentieth century, the first recorded material appeared regarding another scientific conundrum – the effect of the millennium on computer software. It exercised and disturbed minds around the globe. Influential individuals spoke of nasty surprises and dire consequences, which fuelled concerns as the crucial date approached.

The millennium was a unique event in other ways. It was an especially important occasion for families to be able to celebrate it together. Among others, professional seafarers and their families ashore often find themselves far-distant from each other due to work commitments.

At the close of 1999, *Fingal* was manned and on active service. There had been a crew-change two days before Christmas. On board, the millennium proper was also celebrated alongside at Stromness. As well as the local festivities, the NLB's own response to the millennium 'problem' needed to be addressed.

At Stromness Parish Church, in advance of the year-end services and celebrations, the notice board had proclaimed: *Jesus 2000: It's His Millennium*. A rather more dry text had been received on *Fingal*, the Navtex machine printing off its clinical message issued to all ships as a Navigation Navarea Warning:

1ST JAN 2000 IS THE FIRST OF SEVERAL CRITICAL DATES THROUGH 2000 WHEN SOME ELECTRONIC SYSTEMS MAY FAIL DUE TO THEIR INABILITY TO PROCESS THE DATE. SUCH SYSTEMS INCLUDE

AUTOMATION AND SAFETY SYSTEMS WHOSE FAILURE MAY RESULT IN LOSS OF POWER, STEERING OR MALFUNCTIONING OF NAVIGATIONAL OR COMMUNICATIONS EQUIPMENT. MASTERS ARE ADVISED TO CONSIDER CONTINGENCY PLANS IN PREPARATION FOR POSSIBLE FAILURE, TAKING INTO ACCOUNT THE OPERATIONAL PROGRAMME OF THE SHIP. GUIDANCE ON THE RISKS AND PRECAUTIONARY ACTION HAS BEEN PUBLISHED BY THE INTERNATIONAL MARITIME ORGANISATION ...

The millennium problem, with its adopted abbreviation of Y2K, was the subject of internal memoranda issued by the NLB to its ships, which provided checklists and a timetable of events before, during, and after the critical rollover into 1 January 2000:

IMMEDIATELY AFTER ROLLOVER:
1. At 00.30 hrs contact monitor centre with status and any problems that have occurred as a result of the date change. If a problem has occurred that renders the vessel unseaworthy, contact the Operations Manager (Engineering) and (Marine).
2. At 13.00hrs switch back to automatic all machinery previously turned to manual control. Verify all control equipment and navigational against manual systems before relying on automated systems. Items listed should be tested in accordance with the attached test schedule and the results reported to the Operations Manager (Marine) as soon as the tests have been completed ...

There was also very real concern that the computer-based monitoring systems of the NLB's automated lighthouses could be affected. In Orkney, in case all the major lights 'crashed', *Fingal* was on operational standby to position the ship at some pre-selected point to best protect and make safe navigational routes. Such anticipation and state of readiness, as well as the monitoring tasks to be performed, kept a sobering note to the celebratory aspect of the occasion:

Evening: went ashore to get a printed bank balance on my account (in case of Y2K problems!). Rain-soaked streets, glistening flagstones and cobbles throwing up reflections of multi-coloured lights. Deserted. At the Parish Church entrance a board radiated optimism into the quiet emptiness: 'A Hogmanay with a difference. Open 10.00 p.m. for quiet reflection – then "First Footers" welcome.'

Midnight on Fingal: Pre 'rollover' checks carried out. All electronic position inputs recorded. Ship's staff crowded into the small wheelhouse.

Clinton took up station at the ship's bell; Cathryn's hand poised on the lever of the ship's whistle. Glasses charged with amber nectar ... (Author's journal)

As the radio pipped out its message, all hell broke loose: clangings and cheers, handshakes and salutations, the cacophony of ships' whistles and sirens throughout the harbour reverberated about the town, glasses raised to family and absent friends. Welcome to 2000!

CHAPTER 14

Creative Captivity

All ships are a home-away-from-home for their crews. Seafaring is not just a job but a way of life, for crew and their families ashore. Time off-duty while on-board ship represents the equivalent of home life for any crew member. Varied can be the scope of interest and commitment made by any who make up a ship's crew.

On *Fingal*, there was as much self-motivated studying of 'first' language, foreign languages, non-work-related Open University degrees, leisure and academic distance learning, photography, the arts, music, literature and crafts as there was towards further professional advancement.

To native Lewisians from the Outer Hebrides, Gaelic is the language of their birth and colleagues would easily slip into the soft lilt of their mother tongue in the course of private or work-related conversations, where the involvement of others was not needed. A senior officer of Norwegian ancestry tuned into a radio channel to 'keep his hand and ear in'; a coincidence, as a native of north-east England was also studying the language to take advantage of the easy and historic ferry connection across the North Sea, oblivious at the time that this link would soon be permanently severed, rendering his knowledge of the language more academic than of practical use. In a crew cabin along the corridor, tapes of Spanish were being responded to in hushed tones.

It was an unusual privilege to act as official invigilator for a colleague sitting a formal Open University exam, taking a personal break from my own accredited studies in art history. Requiring much reading, suitcases were often weighted with required reading, or the wherewithal to produce working pictures in homage to artists of choice: a landscape of

Francis Towne; a portrait by Max Beckmann. For light relief, a collage encapsulating the work of the Northern Lighthouse Board.

Photography was a medium still based on traditional cameras and film. Some were used in casual fashion; snaps for the family record. A few others applied focused discipline, eager to enjoy the creative process towards a particular goal, and the meticulous record-keeping afterwards. Motivations included national competitions on the broad subject of *Life at Sea*, potential use in the NLB's own *Journal*, exhibition use or in support of articles in nautical magazines or books. This required wearing an additional 'documenter's hat', mindful of the risks of taking expensive equipment into hostile environments to get that elusive encapsulating image.

Music, in its many forms was a pleasure, both passive and active. Engineer Simon Taylor went a step further, applying his fine craftsman skills and technical understanding to make a penny whistle, of soft melodious tone and pitch, out of a rod of extruded plastic. He was generous enough to gift a second instrument to a colleague who appreciated his efforts.

Fingal was essentially based at Stromness in Orkney. An understanding librarian at the local library nearby was sympathetic to pleas for an

Third Engineer Simon Taylor
enjoying musical relaxation.
(Author's Collection)

Some tools of the scumbling wood-graining art: courtesy of Paul Robinson. (Author's Collection)

extraordinary membership and, with it, the leeway of books being returned late because of operational circumstances. A source of many non-fiction titles about the history of maritime and coastal Scotland proved an ideal adjunct to a biographer of the work of *Fingal*.

Manual crafts are applied as part of work requirements, but the detail and quality of finish can be elevated above normal expectation – *if a job is worth doing it is worth doing well* – and brings with it personal satisfactions. The brass telegraphs on the bridge-wings were lovingly buffed; detailing of paintwork was not ignored. For those with the scumbling skills of rendering steel surfaces with the illusion of wood graining in fine panels, *Fingal* and her sister ship provided great scope, to the edification of all who sailed on them.

The following of sport on the media was a given for devotees. Rarely have I been a witness to such an unabashed, primeval outpouring of joy in the Hebridean scream of 'Yes', accompanied by a leaping to the feet and a punch fit to pass through the deckhead above. This was by an ardent supporter watching the final of the UEFA Cup between Manchester United and Bayern Munich, scoring a home equaliser in the short minutes of injury time. Yet this was as a whisper when miraculously the winning second goal followed on. The transformation was complete, from dejection to elation, as victory was snatched from the incredulous jaws of defeat. On the television

Fingal at home at the NLB depot, Stromness, Orkney. (Author's Collection)

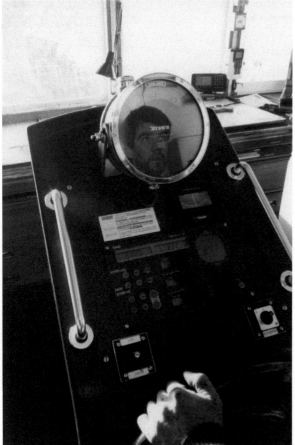

Above: Stromness: a busy depot in a picturesque setting. (Author's Collection)

Left: 'Steady so': helmsman Iain MacNee keeps a sure hand on the wheel. (Author's Collection)

Captain Alan Røre monitors the charted position prior to *Fingal* passing beneath the Forth Rail Bridge. (Author's Collection)

Some tools of the navigator's art: traditional and modern. (Author's Collection)

CalMac ferry *Isle of Arran*, bound for Kennacraig from Port Askaig, passes *Fingal* servicing Black Rock buoy in the Sound of Islay. (Author's Collection)

Above: Second Officer Donald MacLeod repairing a solar buoy cluster lantern. (Author's Collection)

Left: In-situ adjustment of the flashing phase of an acetylene-powered buoy. (Author's Collection)

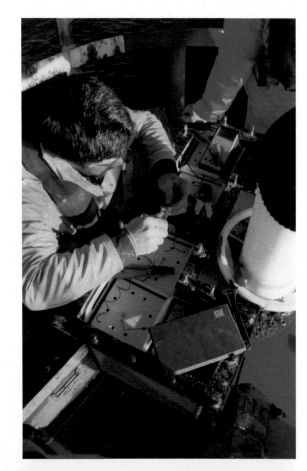

Right: Seaman Iain MacNee effects an in-situ repair to a 'Racon' radar responder unit. (Author's Collection)

Below: A masterpiece of contemporary art: the main deck area where buoys were serviced and repainted. (Author's Collection)

Left: Off Arnish Point, Stornoway: Second Officer Donald MacLeod controls the deck capstan during buoyage operations. (Author's Collection)

Below: At Dundee: taking aboard from a low-loader two new solar cardinal buoys for the Firth of Forth. (Author's Collection)

Above: Awaiting loading: the memorial buoy marking the wreck of HMS *Royal Oak* in Scapa Flow, Orkney. (Author's Collection)

Right: Attending storm damage to the Abertay High Focal Plane buoy. (Author's Collection)

Hydrographic survey work by *Fingal's* workboat off Oban depot pier. (Author's Collection)

Recovering the inflatable after completing local light inspections in Shetland. (Author's Collection)

Duty done: Captain Eric Smith proceeds on leave, by ship's launch into Aberdeen harbour. (Author's Collection)

Orkney ferry *Earl Thorfinn,* inbound for Kirkwall, passes the team inspecting Skerry of Vasa beacon. (Author's Collection)

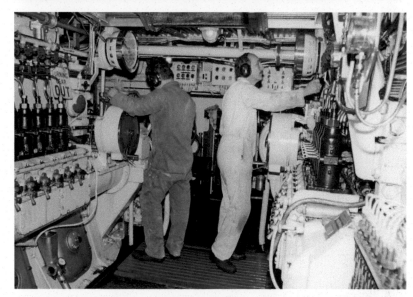

Engine room 'Standby': local manual control of *Fingal's* two main engines, as directed by telegraphs from the bridge. (Author's Collection)

Chief Engineer Robert (Robin) Williamson and Second Engineer Bob Hutton test local control of the emergency steering. (Author's Collection)

Above: A misty morn at Oban depot. (Author's Collection)

Left: Chief Officer John Ross refreshes his skills with a cutting torch. (Author's Collection)

After heavy weather, hosing off salt encrustation to *Fingal*'s superstructure. (Author's Collection)

Sedco 714 semi-submersible 'flaring off'. (Author's Collection)

In drydock: all is revealed. (Author's Collection)

Above: Smoko in the officers' mess: a haven from drydock mayhem. (Author's Collection)

Left: Room with a view: now where are we? (Author's Collection)

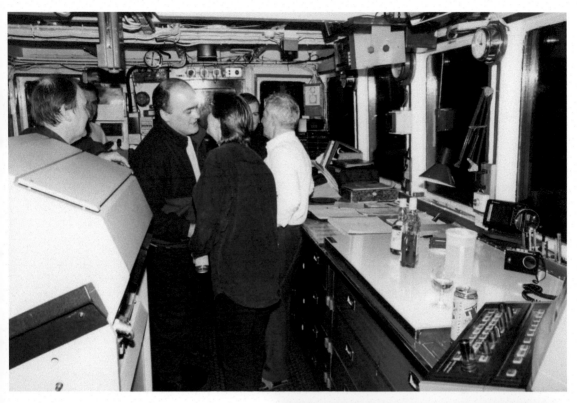

Above: Welcome to the Millennium! (Author's Collection)

Right: Home-from-home: the author's cosy cabin. (Author's Collection)

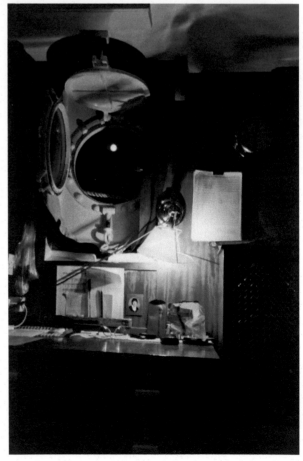

Above: The aft deckhouse displayed the artistry of wood-graining scumble work, done by off-duty crew. (Author's Collection)

Left: Two 'Fine-Gals' finally meet! On *Fingal*, Karen, the author's wife, awaits the launching ceremony of *Fingal's* successor, the *Pole Star*. (Author's Collection)

A celebration birthday cake for the author, made by Karen, his wife. (Author's Collection)

Fingal takes her final leave of Stromness. (Collection of Crispin Worthington)

Delivery voyage to Cornwall. On watch, the author takes *Fingal* south through the Sound of Islay. (Collection of Alan Provan)

Delivery complete: under new ownership, *Fingal*'s delivery crew bade her farewell on the River Fal, Cornwall. (Author's Collection)

Second Officer Donald MacLeod on domestic relaxation after finishing a three-hour Open University examination. (Author's Collection)

The late Alick John Macleod: seaman and stalwart of the Northern Lighthouse Board. (Author's Collection)

Catering department staff Ian Alexander and Cathryn Moir prepare ship for an occasion. (Author's Collection)

The universal routines of washing and ironing. (Author's Collection)

In-house training: Second Officer Donald MacLeod berths *Fingal* at NLB Pier, Oban. (Author's Collection)

A carved miniature tribute of *Fingal*, by Crispin Worthington, proudly displayed at the family guesthouse in Stromness. (Author's Collection)

Ship visit: local resident Crispin Worthington looks on as his grandson Joe takes a bearing with *Fingal*'s gyro compass repeater. (Author's Collection)

screen, stunned disbelief hung heavily on the faces of the other team and their numbed supporters: expressions not held by those assembled in the officer's cabin to share in the spectacle. The pursuit of listening to cricket was generally a more philosophical pastime.

The NLB is active in supporting professional training of cadets under a national scheme. On *Fingal*, a cadet on placement followed the time-honoured path of on-the-job training, coincident with academic study and full-time periods at nautical college. Others, already qualified as seamen, made the admirable commitment to continue their own path towards obtaining officer qualifications, studying hard at the end of their working days.

CHAPTER 15

Dates with *Britannia*

On occasion, *Fingal* was honoured to accompany the Royal Yacht *Britannia* in Scottish waters during official royal visits.

In August 1991, during that year's annual summer cruise of Scotland, the Queen visited Fort William as part of the tercentenary celebrations of the town. Located at the head of Loch Linnhe, north of Oban, *Fingal* escorted the Royal Yacht to Fort William. 8 miles to the south, the loch is constricted by the notable Corran Narrows, which is traversed by vehicle ferry for access to Morvern and Ardnamurchan.

Fingal took up her lead position to the south of Corran Narrows and led *Britannia* and an accompanying Royal Navy warship into upper Loch Linnhe and onwards to Fort William. *Fingal* anchored off the town while royal engagements ashore and members of the Family came and went. Some officers from *Britannia* paid a visit to *Fingal*. On completion, the convoy was led southwards to a point north of the Narrows, where *Fingal* broke away to allow the Royal Yacht and her naval escort to proceed.

In July 1996, *Fingal* provided a short escort into the head of Loch Ryan in southwest Scotland. On at least two other occasions, *Fingal* carried out escort duties at the Isle of Man, and Aberdeen.

CHAPTER 16

Successor

On 9 April 1999, a press release was issued from the headquarters of the NLB in Edinburgh:

The Northern Lighthouse Board is pleased to announce that an order to build a new Aids-to-Navigation Tender has been placed with Ferguson Shipbuilders Limited, of Port Glasgow.

This new Aids-to-Navigation Tender, planned for delivery in September 2000, is designed as a highly manoeuvrable, capable and versatile workhorse. Prime roles will be the maintenance and repair of navigation buoys and beacons, and support routine maintenance of the Northern Lighthouse Board's 200 automatic lighthouses. Strength and sea-keeping necessary to sustain year round operations around the Scottish coastline are key features of the design. Diesel-electric propulsion, dynamic positioning, state-of-the-art navigation and buoy-handling equipment will allow safe handling and precise positioning of aids to navigation in support of all mariners.

The new vessel, as yet unnamed, will replace MV FINGAL (built 1963) and will supplement the capabilities of the Board's other vessel, MV PHAROS (built 1993). It will also be available to operate around the British Isles coast on an interchange basis with the three vessels operated by Trinity House Lighthouse Service and the Commissioners of Irish Lights.

The contract was awarded in the face of stiff competition. The new vessel will provide the most cost-effective solution to the requirements of the Board as the General Lighthouse Authority for Scotland and the Isle of Man.

Following an internal consultation process, the name of the new tender was chosen to be *Pole Star* – the fourth NLB vessel to carry the name. *Pole Star (III)* had been the capable sister ship to *Fingal*.

Fingal's crew were to find themselves directly transferred to her new-build high-tech replacement. Both *Fingal* and her crew were present on the Clyde for the new ship's launching by HRH The Princess Royal, Patron of the Northern Lighthouse Board. The eventual rapid transition by *Fingal*'s crew saw the adoption of entirely new modes of ship operations, very much of the twenty-first century.

The building of any new ship of specialist design and purpose, aimed at replacing an earlier generation of vessel and at integrating it into role, is a complex business that exercises many minds over a considerable length of time. A year would pass since the official press release encapsulated the reality of *Fingal*'s successor for her to be launched bearing the traditional name *Pole Star*.

Throughout this period *Fingal* and her crews continued work as normal but, inevitably, with an eye to the future in all the departments. Several weeks before the launch date, on *Fingal* matters had resolved to the finer details:

> 10 March 2000: In preparation for the launch of *Pole Star*, the shortfall in uniforms is being addressed. In the cabin, behind the closed door, Clinton submits to a colleague wielding a piece of string to measure the finer points of anatomy for a good fit, guided by the tailor's diagrams. Across the desk, an outstretched steel tape measure confirms the size: to either chagrin, or relief! (Author's journal)

Fingal's crew had changed in Stromness six days before the launch of *Pole Star*. She carried out buoy work at Ullapool, discharged defunct buoys at Oban depot for scrap, before proceeding south via the notable Gulf of Corryvreckan for a night anchorage in the Sound of Gigha, to the west of the Mull of Kintyre. The following day the ship made passage for the Clyde, arriving mid-afternoon at Ocean Terminal, Greenock.

An occasion was clearly in the offing as, astern of *Fingal*, *Pharos* also berthed alongside. Like the latest *Pole Star*, she, too, had been built at Ferguson's yard, and was launched into the Clyde in 1993. At that time, she represented a dramatic change in concept from her namesake predecessor, which had come out of a similar classic design stable to that of *Fingal*.

A succinct log entry summed up the pomp, ceremony and celebrations of 6 April 2000:

LAUNCH OF MV POLE STAR AT FERGUSON'S YARD, PORT GLASGOW, BY HRH PRINCESS ANNE [1250hrs]. RECEPTION AT ERSKINE BRIDGE HOTEL.

Apart from the few volunteers who remained to look after *Fingal* at her tidal berth, the ship's complement trooped across the gangway in all their uniformed finery, to the awaiting coach. Morning commuters on the railway linking Glasgow Central station to Gourock would have seen, on passing Port Glasgow, a heavy presence of yellow-clad police at the entrance to the shipyard. Within the yard itself, a festive atmosphere prevailed: a chatting, milling crowd, with the crews of both ships unusually all together and united with their families, who had also 'scrubbed up well'.

The dockworkers, in yellow hard hats and boiler suits, were quietly proud of their latest achievement, which loomed large and sat perkily as the centre of attention. Adjacent, the red-primed pre-fabricated bulk of the latest ferry of CalMac's Western Isles fleet was taking shape. I had no idea that, a decade later, I would be serving on this ship – the *Hebrides* – on her route linking Skye, North Uist, and Harris.

A pipe band added to the festiveness, the tight crescent and backdrop of high buildings enhancing the acoustics. Office staff with an elevated vantage peered at windows, mugs of drinks in hand. On the roof hovered the police and the press. A hush descended, marking the arrival of HRH The Princess Royal who, in the additional capacity of Patron of the Northern Lighthouse Board, was to launch *Pole Star*.

After the ship was blessed, there followed the anticipated awkward pause before *Pole Star* began to move. Gathering silent momentum, all too quickly it seemed, she slid into her element. Much cheering and tossing of hats would have disguised discreet sighs of relief. Greeted raucously with blaring whistles by the awaiting tugs, the ship was turned broadside at the top of the tide before being towed to the fitting-out berth.

Upstream, near the Erskine Bridge, the hotel that hosted the reception revealed a fine prospect from its windows: the mighty river, Dumbarton Rock, and the channel buoys and substantial beacons that lead to a formerly important port near the heart of Glasgow city itself. All those present were currently involved in witnessing the latest increment of an extraordinary maritime history on the banks of Clyde.

CHAPTER 17

Fond and Fitting Farewells

The replacement of *Fingal*, and her withdrawal and sale out of NLB service, was necessarily widely known long in advance. This provided many opportunities for a range of acknowledgements and expressions of fond farewells. Suddenly, there was the poignant realisation that an era was fast approaching its conclusion, and that 'the last of her type' would sail finally beyond the horizon, taking a wealth of associations and memories with her.

> 29 April 2000: Depart Tayside; Year 2000 work completed. At Tay Bar outward, reported to Dundee Harbour by radio that this was the final scheduled visit by *Fingal*, casualty work excepted. This lack of ceremony began the process of 'withdrawal'. (Author's journal)

At Stornoway, in mid-June, the knowledge of her ultimate call found the families of crew visiting. Discerning holidaymakers – mature couples consuming chips – paused to admire. Making enquiries, there followed a sense of disappointment on hearing that *Fingal* did not carry passengers.

Ship visits were made by prospective buyers, each mentally imposing their own required concepts on the reality of the vessel as found. Ship's staff found themselves in the uneasy position as proxy seller's agents: loyal supporters saddened at the commercial constraints of 'market value'. In preparation for transfer of ownership, the tasks of generating lists of sundry stores, equipment, and the lengthy accumulation of spares, occupied many a concentrated hour. Small 'souvenir' items were labelled and removed to 'safety'!

The impact on ship's personnel of *Fingal's* replacement had started a year previously:

> On the bridge, Sandy – a Shetlander and former NLB Lighthouse Keeper – rattled off the names of the tall lighthouses around the Orkneys at which he had served: 'In those days it was a huge job, painting the towers: all ropes and chairs and head for heights'. Now Sandy is a Welfare Adviser, sailing on *Fingal* to apprise the crew about the consequences of manning changes when the new *Pole Star* enters service, and the packages and options open to them. (Author's journal)

In 1993, *Fingal's* sister ship *Pole Star* took her final leave from Stromness and NLB service. The occasion was captured on amateur video by an NLB engineer-donkeyman. In advance of *Fingal's* own departure, the video was shown on board; the effect it had on the riveted viewers was a precursor to the later event, now fast approaching. It was a fine day when *Pole Star* slipped her berth to pirouette in the harbour confines and head for the entrance. The video silence was broken by two sets of five blasts on the ship's whistle. Her form diminished as she sailed down Clestrain Sound towards Scapa Flow, and onward to a very different future.

On 9 August 2000, a log entry stated simply:

> 1806 hours: FINAL DEPARTURE FROM STROMNESS: Passage to Oban …

The flag hoist of her call sign – GMJA – flew tautly at the foremast's starboard halyard. As *Fingal* backed away stern-first from the depot pier, she gave her customary manoeuvring whistle signal of three short blasts, which gently echoed from the gable-ends of the houses nearby. On the private stone pier of a waterfront guest house with a commanding view of the harbour, a lone piper provided a fitting and poignant tribute, which cut through the wind and reached *Fingal*: a plaintive and rending farewell. At the harbour entrance, she swung boldly to the west, disappearing from view. Feeling once again the tidal stream of Hoy Mouth and the lift of the Atlantic swell, *Fingal* made passage for Cape Wrath and an overnight steam towards Oban.

Finally taking leave of Oban with its principal depot and long associations with the town, fervently waved white towels of anonymous admirers signalled their own poignant farewells. Soon afterwards, across the airways from a seaborne location nearby came a discreet, timely and gratifying message from the NLB's Patron, HRH The Princess Royal: '*Fingal* – God speed'. In a subsequent edition of the in-house NLB magazine, *The Journal,* Princess Anne gave a message to the master and crew, MV *Fingal*:

> It is with sadness that I learned of MV *Fingal's* departure from the Northern Lighthouse Service. In my time as Patron, I look back on many happy days spent onboard *Fingal* around the coast of Scotland, seeing for myself your professionalism and seamanship in your essential work in support of all seagoers. I wish the ship a long, prosperous and honourable retirement in private use, and to Master and Crew my thanks and very best wishes for the future.

As the voyage to the south coast of England began, similar words were recalled at the launching of *Fingal's* successor: 'May God bless all who sail in her.' Princess Anne had voiced the traditional hope, and welcome for the new *Pole Star.* When the latest ship for the NLB had entered the Clyde amid general cheers, the raising of white caps from the uniformed officers and crews crystallised those simple and compelling words. To them, this vessel would become a new workplace and home.

Looking ahead with anticipation inevitably causes a backward glance. Some thirty-seven years previously, another new ship had slid into those same waters; an earlier generation of mariners would have raised their caps in welcome to *Fingal*, and contemplated how her future would unfold. Little could they guess how her final crew would come to cherish the official *Fingal* stamp in their discharge books.

Fingal was as cutting-edge in her youth as the sharpness of her fine bow, which made light of boisterous head seas. She easily shrugged off the more recent affectionate gibe of being 'state of the ark' by her sea-kindly grace, trustworthy simplicity and essential elegance.

Leaning at the broad wooden rails was a defining way to appreciate the myriad beauties of the Scottish coasts, which were enhanced by her presence. Labours of pride endured in the scumbled wood-graining art to the deckhouses and bulwarks. In the restored gleaming splendour of brass telegraphs, the reflection of a watchman's face revealed the daily satisfaction of a job well done.

Over her bridge-wing dodgers hung the echoes of buoy work and the banter that makes light of wielding heavy hatch boards and winter-stiff tarpaulins; the cut-throat signal to the bridge that all is done. In the wooden-decked alleyway, lit by the timeless warm glow of tungsten, a pattern of glossy wet footprints between the shared shower room and cabin would confirm end of work for yet another day. In the saloon, the crested silver teapot was ever ready with a refill; in the engine room

Fingal celebrated on an Isle of Man postage stamp. (Author's Collection)

the gentle putter of a generator was a companionable and life-long heartbeat.

Such were the reflections that accompanied the quiet outward attentiveness of a navigator on watch, privileged to have been both a part of it, and part of this particular special-delivery voyage.

CHAPTER 18

Special Delivery

When *Fingal* was sold out of service to a private buyer, the ship was delivered by NLB crew for lay-up in the River Fal, in south-west England. Her departure from Scotland was variously celebrated and the passage itself was an unusual experience for those involved, as was the occasion of the official transfer of ownership in the Fal.

Activity at Oban was brisk prior to *Fingal's* delivery voyage. Log entries for August 2000 record:

9th: 09.00: Passage to Ardnamurchan: lay Experimental Buoy. 16.45: berth at Oban.

10th: 08.36: Leave berth to allow *Pharos* alongside. Transfer excess bunkers to *Pharos*. Transfer ex-*Fingal* stores and equipment to *Pharos* and Oban Depot. Leave berth to allow *Pharos* to sail. 16.18: Secure alongside.

11th: Continue offloading to depot. 12.00–16.00: *Fingal* and depot open to the public.

12th: Continue offloading to depot. Anticipated buyer of *Fingal* and representatives aboard.

Fingal took final leave of Oban on 13 August, making passage as she had so often done via the Sound of Kerrera, the buoys of its convoluted channels well known to her tender care. This narrow and sheltered defile hides a notable history:

It closes the bay at Oban, and is itself rich in famous harbours. In one of these assembled the Scots fleet of Alexander II when his expedition was fitting out against the Hebrides. Almost exactly seven hundred years later, in the same place, a fleet of Coastal Command Short Sunderlands would be assembling and operating over half the Atlantic, with the Sound of Kerrera as its war base. All the sea-kings and admirals who have had business in the western waters have known the four miles length of Kerrera.

Clearing the sheltered waters and sailing with a reduced delivery crew, *Fingal* lifted her bows to the rumour of an Atlantic swell as the brass telegraph rang melodiously, 'Full away!'

As per the detailed passage plan (see Appendix 3), *Fingal* took leave of the Sound of Islay, the Mull of Kintyre and North Channel, transiting the Irish Sea to the lanes of the Traffic Separation Scheme off Pembrokeshire, and braced the Atlantic fringe of the Bristol Channel towards the tip of the Cornish Peninsula. Adjusting her speed for a timed arrival at Falmouth pilot station, the night-time navigation off Land's End was rewarded by the beaming presence of the great lighthouses, whose very names were an inspiration.

> Wolf flashed to Round Island; Lizard loomed towards Bishop ...
> They winked at each other,
> As brother to brother,
> Those red lights and white lights, the summer night through.

From *The Ballad of the Royal Ann* by Crosbie Garstin

These were foreign waters to *Fingal*, but the Cornish sea lights saluted her with a guiding welcome. Rounding the peninsula with customary style, she felt the rake of Lizard's sweeping beams and a swell under the stern, as her speed was eased.

In the cool of morning twilight, the unusual event of boarding a pilot took place off St Anthony's Head. It was with an inquisitive interest that the winding buoyed channel was followed across broad Carrick Roads. Dawn brought both stillness and colour to the constricting reaches of the River Fal that closed intimately on either side, with ancient oakwoods to the very shore. Beyond King Harry Ferry, a clutch of laid-up reefer ships left scant room for passage.

In the wheelhouse, the plan for manoeuvring and mooring was outlined by the pilot. *Fingal* was to berth alongside *Tamamima*, an ex-Bank Line

A quiet passage up the River Fal. (Author's Collection)

A quiet passage up the River Fal. (Author's Collection)

freighter of traditional mould, moored as yet out of sight, but just around the next right-angled bend. Anticipation was acute.

'There is deep water right up to the banks,' reassured the pilot, as *Fingal* pirouetted to face downstream. Astern and rearing high in her light-ship condition, *Tamamima* dominated the river. *Fingal*'s anchors plunged into the umber depths. 'Don't let any weight come on either anchor,' urged the pilot as, with a slow but practised certainty, *Fingal* made sternway. The harbourmaster's boat fussed busily, running long lines to the mooring buoys. High above, on *Tamamima*'s main deck, her skeleton foreign crew hauled up the ropes.

As the telegraphs were rung to 'Finish with engines' and answered with echoing finality, regret and pride settled with the silence: for both *Fingal* and crew, it was a good job done.

Edging past other laid-up ships. (Author's Collection)

Fingal secure alongside *Tamamima*. (Author's Collection)

CHAPTER 19

What's in a Name?

The word 'Fingal' comes from the Irish *Fine Gall*, meaning 'foreign tribe'. It is a county in Ireland, derived from the medieval Viking settlement, north of Dublin.

Fingal's Cave is a famous feature on the uninhabited island of Staffa, lying to the west of the Isle of Mull, in the Inner Hebrides of Scotland. It is owned by the National Trust for Scotland. The cave is formed entirely from hexagonally jointed basalt columns, similar in structure to the Giant's Causeway in Northern Ireland. It became known as Fingal's Cave after the eponymous hero of an epic poem by eighteenth-century Scots poet-historian James Macpherson. In Irish mythology, the hero is known as *Fionn mac Cumhaill*. It has been suggested that Macpherson rendered the name as Fingal, meaning 'white stranger'. The legend of the Giant's Causeway has 'Fingal' building it between Ireland and Scotland.

The cave's size, its naturally arched roof and the eerie sounds produced by the echoes of waves give it the atmosphere of a cathedral. The German composer Mendelssohn visited Fingal's Cave during a tour of Scotland. It inspired him to compose the concert overture *The Hebrides*, also known as *Fingal's Cave*. Mendelssohn himself labelled the score as such.

As a name for ships, 'Fingal' is not unique, but there has only been one *Fingal* built for the Northern Lighthouse Board. After her replacement, the name was transferred to the workboat of the new ship.

Windsor Castle is the oldest and largest occupied castle in the world and is an official Royal residence. William the Conqueror chose the site high above the River Thames, intended to guard the western approaches to London.

The Royal Mail Ship *Windsor Castle* was the largest passenger-cargo liner operated by the famous Union-Castle Line on its service between Britain and South Africa. The vessel was to be the last flagship of the line and, briefly, the largest liner built in England.

Windsor Castle was sold out of service in 1977, an occasion that marked the end of the era of regular ocean-liner services to and from Africa. The renamed ship fulfilled other roles under Greek ownership. Prior to being scrapped on the remote beaches of Alang in India, a strong preservation movement had aims to save the famous liner. Part of this ambitious and noble scheme was the retention of her original name. It is understood that the former *Fingal* was renamed *Windsor Castle* by her new owner with this in mind.

In January 2016, the ship had her original name formally restored to her. *Fingal* was painted on each bow and at the stern.

CHAPTER 20

Northbound Again!

Fingal – in her reincarnated guise as *Windsor Castle* – spent fourteen years moored in the pristine environs of the River Fal. Maintained throughout in good order by her private owner, outwardly the ship took on a modified livery. Her masts, derricks and crane became dazzling white, as did the beautifully wood-grained deckhouses. The funnel assumed a yellow hue.

The vessel became a known and admired part of the river scenery, which, in itself, is widely known and loved. One day in August 2014, the prospect changed: *Windsor Castle* left, for good.

To prepare the ship, she was first towed to Falmouth drydock by the tug *St Piran,* with *Percuil* acting as brakes at the stern. After power-washing 25 tonnes of mussels off the hull, the insurance company had her surveyed and the necessary works required for the tow north were undertaken.

Her departure was reported in the *Falmouth Packet* newspaper, which indicated that the Falmouth and Brixham-based Marine & Towage Services' latest tug *Vanguard,* then only two months old, paid a fleeting visit to Falmouth to tow *Windsor Castle* to Leith. Described as a Shoalbuster tug with a bollard pull of 50 tonnes, she represents a highly capable modern craft. New and old had been brought together for a voyage where admiration and respect became mutual.

The appointed owner's representative of *Windsor Castle,* former Falmouth pilot Gordon Kent, was not only an authority on local navigable waters but, after retirement, served as skipper on tugs of the same company as *Vanguard.* Responsibility for the safe transit of *Vanguard* and her unpowered charge fell in turn to four successive pilots before the open water of Falmouth Bay was reached.

Ahead lay a passage through some of the most congested coastal waters in the world. A tug-and-tow brings with it demands and constraints on manoeuvring and the regard that may need to be given by other classes of sea-going craft. By day, the special status of *Vanguard* and *Windsor Castle* was given visual reinforcement by particular shapes hoisted on halyards and, in the hours of darkness, additional navigation lights in accordance with the 'Col-Regs' – the International Regulations for the Prevention of Collision at Sea – the primary code governing the behaviour and interaction of all craft at sea.

In the course of the voyage, tug-and-tow would make copious reference to many fundamental navigation aids that were the stuff of the working life of *Fingal*, although for most of the transit they were provided by Trinity House: a variety of buoy types, lightvessels and lighthouses now long unmanned and automatic, and the invisible high technology of electronic positioning systems. After the testing constriction of the Dover Straits, the big 'left-hand turn' eventually allowed northerly courses into the North Sea proper.

In the morning twilight of 22 August, tug-and-tow was shaping a course off the Northumberland coast to clear the Farne Islands. The welcoming beam of Longstone Lighthouse greeted the two vessels to the south, its distinctive red and white tower throwing back the morning sun as they passed. After the holy island of Lindisfarne and the border town of Berwick-upon-Tweed, Scottish waters beckoned. A span of years has passed but *Fingal* was once again home!

It was pure serendipity that, perchance, my wife and I may have been the first land-based souls to recognise and indeed welcome *Fingal* back to her home territory. It was the instinct of a lifetime's professional preoccupation as a ship's bridge watchkeeper to seek and ascertain what other vessels were in the area. Viewed at a distance from the harbour of St Abb's, and materialising slowly from the run of sea and the sunlit white caps, the general configuration of a tug-and-tow resolved itself. As to the vessel being towed, despite an apparent change of livery which in no way tricked the deeply ingrained knowledge of the ship, it dawned on us that *Fingal* was indeed there in front of us and, evidently, making good speed.

Binoculars brought to bear, and to share, confirmed what I already knew was certainty. To add further to the drama and excitement, another northbound vessel hove into view: none other than *Fingal's* successor, the 'new' *Pole Star*, quite literally in *Fingal's* wake.

The duty master of *Pole Star*, Neil MacLean, recalls the background to the occasion:

We surveyed the area around the Longstone Lighthouse at the Farne Islands as there was to be major work done on the light. Trinity House was looking to temporarily substitute it with a lightvessel. They had identified a good location and we surveyed it to make sure there were no obstructions. We also landed 9,000 litres of diesel to the light using the attendant's boat. He worked out of nearby Seahouses and his boat had tanks, which we filled. He then pumped it ashore at the landing. We also did some buoy work further south, all the way down to Bridlington. On heading back to the Forth we overhauled *Fingal* off St Abb's Head.

As the tug-and-tow continued its slow trend to a more westerly course in anticipation of the outer approaches to the Firth of Forth, it passed the grey modern scar of Torness nuclear power station. Nearing the Lothian town of Dunbar with its tall outlier lighthouse at Barns Ness, the unusual outfall buoy tucked into the bay at Belhaven passed unnoticed on this occasion; as would the location of experimental buoys historically laid by *Fingal* between Bass Rock and the coast. To the north, was the Isle of May with its

The tug MTS *Vanguard* and *Windsor Castle* prior to the tow from the River Fal to Leith. (Collection of MTS, Falmouth)

200-year-old lighthouse, and beyond, the great Inchcape guardian of Bell Rock Lighthouse, known of old. Off North Berwick, the demure island of Fidra, with its sea-swallow colony of terns, also soon passed astern.

Vanguard handed over the towing bridle to Forth Ports' tug *Fidra*, with *Seal Carr* in support, to take *Windsor Castle* through the lock gates at Leith and to her holding berth at Prince of Wales Dock.

Fulfilling this special delivery, *Vanguard* headed not only south, but to the Deep South, for a lengthy charter in South American waters. *Fingal* had essentially completed a circumnavigation of the British mainland, albeit over a period of fourteen years. But absence makes the heart grow fonder.

As Bob Downie, chief executive of the RY *Britannia* at Leith Docks, observed the arrival of *Fingal*, he recalled the events of the previous six years, which had made it all happen ...

CHAPTER 21

How It All Happened,
by Bob Downie

Just before Christmas 2008, I met our chairman, Rear Admiral Neil Rankin CB CBE, for a coffee in Edinburgh's Balmoral Hotel, and he handed me a letter from a Mr Mark Bamford of the intriguingly named Tamahine Investments Ltd of Deanery Street, Mayfair, London. As I read the letter, I advised my chairman that the subject matter, MV *Windsor Castle*, was a beautiful vessel with classic lines and we should travel to Cornwall to view her. However, I had no inclination that we would then spend much of the next five-and-a-half years negotiating our acquisition of a vessel, better known to me as *Fingal*, that I had very fond memories of seeing regularly as I grew up in Oban. Indeed, for many years, I could see in the far distance the Fingal Pier, as it is still known today, from my family home until a new terrace of apartments blocked our view of Oban Bay.

Returning to my office on *Britannia*, I Googled the Deanery Street address, and was surprised to find it was also the London address of JCB. Further online investigations were to reveal that Mr Bamford was the second son of the late Joseph Cyril Bamford, founder of the iconic JCB excavators firm. At first glance, Mr Bamford was seeking to find an appropriate new home for a vessel of which he had become very fond, and had probably spent over a million pounds lovingly maintaining, since he originally took ownership in 2000. On reflection, the time it took to conclude the deal was perhaps elongated by his understandable reluctance to part with such a beautiful ship.

In the early years of our negotiations, there was no direct flight from Edinburgh to Newquay airport in Cornwall, but we could do so from Glasgow. So, in the spring of 2009, off went our chairman, myself, and

Derek Miller, the naval architect in charge of *Britannia's* maintenance. After picking up our hire car at Newquay airport, better known to Admiral Rankin from his naval aviator 'Blue Diamond' display-team days as RAF St Mawgan, we headed to Truro railway station to meet one of Mr Bamford's ship surveyors, Peter Curtis. After locating Mr Curtis, we stopped at the local supermarket to purchase some provisions for our buffet lunch, before setting off to see *Fingal* for the first time in twenty-odd years. Thanks to Mr Curtis' prior warning, I successfully negotiated the unusually dangerous 'figure of eight' small roundabout on the way out of Truro. The first thing that struck me about being in 'rural' Cornwall was that it had three-lane motorways, an early indication of just how popular the area was in the summer months, attracting more annual visitors than Scotland.

Before long we had turned off the main-road network and were driving past the National Trust's Trelissick Gardens on our way to King Harry's Ferry, the chain ferry originally dating from 1888 that links St Mawes with the Roseland Peninsula, saving a 27-mile journey. Just past Trelissick, Mr Curtis finally got a signal on his phone, allowing him to instruct the crew of *Windsor Castle* to send a boat to collect us at the rather aptly named Smugglers' Cottage. It was my first crossing on a chain ferry and, as it noisily tugged itself across the River Fal, we eagerly looked for an early sight of the reason we were here, but none was forthcoming. Driving off the ferry and up the very steep hill on the Peninsula side, Mr Curtis advised that on the next right-hand bend we should instead turn sharply left and go down a small single-track road that had been built by the Americans for embarkation for the D-Day landings. After about half a mile, we arrived at the fifteenth-century thatched Smugglers' Cottage, at that time a restaurant but now a family home. Immediately in front of us was *Windsor Castle*, moored alongside and completely dwarfed by a giant laid-up refrigerated cargo ship.

Despite having the privilege of being in charge of one of the most iconic ships in the world, I could never be described as a 'ship-spotter'. However, seeing *Fingal* again after all these years, albeit now with *Windsor Castle* painted on her side, in these surreal surroundings on the River Fal, quickly reminded me of what a beautiful vessel she was, thus strengthening our resolve to try and acquire her. At a fairly derelict jetty adjacent to Smugglers' Cottage sat one of the former Northern Lighthouse Board workboats, now crewed by two Ukrainians, who were to take us the 200 or so metres to board the vessel.

As we climbed up the accommodation ladder, Mr Bamford was there to meet us, accompanied by Mr John McMinn, another of his ship surveyors.

After pleasantries were exchanged, Mr Bamford put on his white boiler suit and proceeded to give us a tour of the vessel. We were immediately impressed by the maintenance regime he had in place, including having the engines turned over every month. He explained that, in the summer months, he had a crew of five constantly maintaining the vessel and, in the winter months, there was a crew of three, even though it had not sailed one inch since it was originally delivered to him by the NLB in 2000. Below decks there was an eerie haunting feel, as if the NLB crew had simply stepped ashore, with all their equipment still where they left it, which reminded me of my first moments on *Britannia* back in May 1998. After our tour, including seeing the splendid engine room, we sat in the former Commissioners' Lounge and, over a cold buffet lunch, learned of Mr Bamford's plans to dispose of the vessel now that he had abandoned his original idea to lengthen the vessel and turn it into a private yacht. Once we had concluded our initial discussions, the ex-NLB workboat took us back to shore and we retraced our steps to King Harry's Ferry, and on to our hotel.

That evening, over dinner in the local Premier Inn, we agreed that it was a project worth pursuing. Our thoughts turned to how best to undertake our due diligence, with the condition of the hull being foremost in our minds, since it had been nine years since a drydock survey was last undertaken. The following day, before flying home, we drove to Padstow to see the National Lobster Hatchery, as Admiral Rankin was then also the chairman of the Scottish Seabird Centre in North Berwick. They were undertaking a feasibility study to consider setting up a similar facility, although sadly it never proceeded despite its very obvious appeal, both from a marine ecological perspective and for boosting the attraction's popularity and viability. My final memory of our first trip to Cornwall was, however, the very unusual £5 exit fee everyone had to pay at Newquay airport before being allowed into the departure lounge. This was a local tax being collected by the council as part of their attempts to develop the airport; a commendable objective, but a very strange last memory of my first visit to Cornwall!

Despite our obvious enthusiasm to acquire another classic ship, the key question was, 'what would we do with her?' A review of the numbers visiting small heritage ships in Scotland quickly dismissed the idea of *Fingal* being a heritage museum alongside *Britannia*, despite this being an obvious idea, and thoughts then turned to a static floating hotel. This would represent organic growth, since *Britannia* already had all the departments you would expect to find in a hotel, although perhaps with different titles: Sales & Marketing, Hospitality & Events, Maintenance & Security, Housekeeping, Finance, HR, etc.

We then commissioned hotel-and-leisure commercial-property consultants GVA to undertake a feasibility study to see if there was merit in such an idea. Their study confirmed that there was ample demand in the Edinburgh hotel market for a small luxury boutique hotel with about twenty bedrooms. The term 'boutique' I was to change over time to 'boatique', as opposed to the more commonly used 'boatel'.

Following this vote of confidence, we returned to Cornwall on several occasions, often accompanied by colleagues who would be involved in either the conversion or operation of the hotel, should the project proceed. Over time, the Glasgow–Newquay flight was withdrawn from service, and our trips to the Fal generally consisted of flying to Exeter, hiring a car, driving down the A30 for about two hours to Truro and then across to King Harry's Ferry. The Edinburgh–Exeter flight landed at noon, with the same plane returning an hour or so later, so our return trip to Edinburgh was generally via Bristol. This gave us the opportunity to visit the excellent *SS Great Britain*, rather spectacularly housed in the drydock that was originally constructed to build Brunel's great ship in 1839.

Negotiating with someone of great personal wealth is probably not something for which my humble Oban upbringing adequately prepared me but, over time, our legal jousts with Mr Bamford became mildly more 'entertaining' – although I am not sure that is a word my chairman, or colleagues, would have used to describe the frustration they often felt. Indeed my sympathies generally lay, not with ourselves, but with JCB's group legal director, who had the unfortunate duty to convey the variations to what we thought had already been agreed only days or weeks before.

After several years of on-off negotiations, we finally reached a point whereby we would pay for the vessel to be drydocked in Falmouth in June 2013. This would then allow the hull to be power-washed of all the marine growth in order for our insurance company to survey the vessel, and assess whether or not it was in a fit state to be towed to Leith. If the survey results were good, the sale would go through and, if the survey results were poor, then we would pay for the hull to be repainted, and for the vessel to be returned to her River Fal berth, and that would be the end of it.

Over time, the Ukrainian maintenance crew had been replaced by a Bulgarian crew led by a very good engineer called Ivan Voronevski, who would meet us with the small NLB workboat at Smugglers' Cottage to take us out to *Windsor Castle*. Just what the Ukrainian, and then Bulgarian, crew made of permanently maintaining in a very good working order a ship that never moved an inch in fourteen years is hard to imagine, although there are many worse places than on the River Fal to sit in the evening, fishing and watching the world go by.

As the drydocking approached, rather than sell the vessel to us, Mr Bamford suggested that he gift the vessel to us, on the proviso that he be able to retain, removed at our cost, various items of equipment, such as the large Welin Crane, Helipad, Russell Newbury emergency generator, and the small boats and davits. Given that they were surplus to our own requirements, and would be removed as part of our proposed conversion, this seemed like a reasonable arrangement and we agreed to this change. It then meant that, if the insurance survey was good, the vessel would then head up to Leith. If it failed the survey, then we would have it towed to Swansea to be broken up.

Unfortunately, the list of items Mr Bamford wished to retain continued to grow. His insistence that some were removed and reassembled in working order created unsurmountable problems that led to him withdrawing his offer a few days before the vessel was due to go into drydock, and we cancelled our flights and accommodation in Cornwall. It was over.

With *Fingal* no longer on our horizon, our attention now turned to sourcing another classic heritage vessel that could be converted into a small hotel. This proved to be a very frustrating process, with most of the classic vessels we identified having already been beached at places like Alang in India for breaking up. Eventually, we found what might be a suitable replacement, a former Chilean Navy patrol vessel, now converted into a small cruise ship and renamed *Antarctic Dream*. It had forty small double cabins and our desk research got as far as considering how to get to the south of Chile for an inspection. In a strange twist, the most direct route to Punta Arenas was by flying to the Falklands, where our own chairman had been commander of the British Armed Forces, immediately following the conflict. As our excitement grew at the prospect of flying from RAF Brize Norton to the Falklands via Ascension Island, coincidently commanded during the conflict by Captain Bob McQueen, Royal Barge Officer on HMY *Britannia* in 1956/57, so too did another realisation. While we may have been in a position to afford to purchase the vessel, we could not afford the cost of the crew and fuel to sail her nearly 8,000 nautical miles back to Leith – reminding me of the old phrase: if you can't afford the petrol, then don't buy the car!

All then went silent until early November 2013, when I was in London to attend a hospitality conference celebrating thirty years of the Catey Awards, the industry's Oscars, having been honoured to win the 2005 Tourism Award. On the morning of the conference, I was walking into the Jumeirah Calton Tower Hotel, when who should I bump into on the pavement but Mr Bamford, strolling towards his offices in Mayfair. After exchanging pleasantries like long-lost chums, we wished each other good day, and I then went inside to meet up with Andrew Thomson, who is head of our Hospitality & Events department and told him of this surprise encounter.

Returning to *Britannia* on Monday, I had an email from Mr Bamford suggesting that we rekindle the original deal, but without the onerous conditions that led to the collapse in June 2013. It was therefore with some trepidation that I suggested to our chairman that we enter into fresh negotiations to secure ownership of *Windsor Castle*. Following some internal debate about the merits of expecting a different outcome this time around, I travelled down to London just before Christmas to meet Mr Bamford at his Mayfair office. On this occasion, I sensed a determination on his part to get the deal done, almost as if he had reluctantly accepted that it was now time to let go of his beloved prized possession.

True to his word, Mr Bamford helped ensure that the legal negotiations passed without incident and we had GVA refresh the business plan once more. To their credit, having done this so many times already in the intervening years, they said they would only invoice us if the project went ahead. We also brought on board Duncan Maclean of Brodies LLP, a specialist maritime lawyer who in 2010 helped *Britannia* purchase the former royal racing yacht *Bloodhound* that was owned by The Queen and Duke of Edinburgh in the 1960s. For interest, *Bloodhound* is now on display alongside *Britannia* apart from in July and August, when it goes to Oban for a day-sailing charter, skippered and crewed primarily by ex-*Britannia* Royal Yachtsmen.

On 15 July 2014, our Derek Miller travelled to the Fal to meet with our insurance company's marine surveyor to do a pre-tow inspection, following which the works they identified would be undertaken prior to the ship going down the river to Falmouth drydock – assuming there were no last-minute surprises. Derek also met up with representatives of A&P Falmouth, who operated the docks to make provisional arrangements for the docking the following week.

It was therefore with a mixture of excitement and trepidation that Andrew Thomson and myself travelled to Cornwall on 22 July hopefully to complete our acquisition of *Windsor Castle* the following day. We again flew to Exeter, picked up the hire car, drove for an hour, stopped at our usual roadside Subway hut for lunch, and arrived in Falmouth in the middle of – by Scottish standards – a heat wave. After dropping off our bags at the hotel, we walked to the drydock for a pre-meeting that had some twenty people in attendance; representatives from the dock company and tug company, harbour masters from the three different 'territories' that *Windsor Castle* would pass through on a very short journey, the pilot, and the 'tow master'. I found this last role to be rather bemusing; having to pay for someone who was technically there as our ship's Captain, but who had, to me, no role to play other than to immediately hand control of this 'dead' ship over to the pilot, a process that we again encountered a few weeks later when *Windsor Castle* arrived in Leith!

Wandering back to the town, we stopped off at the National Maritime Museum Cornwall (NMMC), which I hitherto, and rather naïvely, had thought was an offshoot of the illustrious Greenwich museum of a similar name. It turned out the NMMC had ambitiously adopted this national name as part of a millennium project, and it had no official connection with its virtual namesake. I was keen to see the Dragon Class sailing yacht *Bluebottle*, which was on loan to NMMC from the Duke of Edinburgh.

After a quick look around the museum, we asked a member of staff where *Bluebottle* was. He did not have a clue what we were talking about. I thought this was rather odd given the yacht's ownership and pedigree, having won a bronze medal at the 1956 Melbourne Olympics when on loan to the British team. We received a similar response from the next member of staff, before finally finding someone who knew about *Bluebottle*, although his response took me aback. For the last six or seven years, *Bluebottle* had been out of the water, stored under a tarpaulin in a neighbouring car park, while they raised the £25,000 required to restore her back to her former glory. I was appalled at this state of affairs and, on returning to Edinburgh made a formal approach to NMMC to take over the stewardship and upkeep of this important part of British maritime history. Sadly our offer was declined, yet remains on the table today, should they put the yacht's interest ahead of other considerations.

We then walked along Falmouth harbour to investigate from where the small passenger ferry sailed that could allow it to drop us off at Smugglers' Cottage, or failing that, at Trelissick Gardens the next day. I then received a phone call from the legendary James 'Tiny' Little, former Royal Yachtsman and one of the 'Yotties' who helps with *Bloodhound* in Oban each summer, including letting us use his former Admiralty tender *Dornoch* as a bunkhouse for the crew. 'Tiny' is one of life's truly great characters and, if you ever met him you would not believe that he rowed the Atlantic single-handed in 2005, losing an incredible 9 stone of weight in the process – although thankfully he soon found them again.

The next day we explored more of Falmouth, before heading to the pier to buy our ferry tickets. When I asked if it was possible to buy two tickets to Smugglers' Cottage, his response was, 'why do you want to go there?' – a question that was to be repeated on the ferry itself. At Trelissick, nearly everyone got off the ferry, with a few staying on to complete the journey to

Truro. When reminding the crew member that we wanted off at Smugglers' Cottage, he said he had not forgotten because it was the first time anyone had ever asked to get off there. As we turned the bend in the river, with the heavily forested embankments on either side, we saw *Windsor Castle* for the first time on this trip to Cornwall. Our excitement grew: our acquisition might finally happen!

At the Smugglers' Cottage jetty sat one of the former NLB workboats, and the passenger boat dropped us off at the gable of the pontoon, where we took no more than three strides to step aboard the workboat and greet Ivan once more. As we crossed to *Fingal*, I noticed the accommodation ladder that we previously walked up was gone and, instead, a rather worn rope pilot ladder was hanging over the side. A smiling Mr Bamford greeted us from above and I passed up my satchel containing the essential paperwork, and two bottles of Betty Ann Cundall's award-winning Chateau de Charbert's pink fizz, which is bottled under a *Britannia* label. Exchanging formalities with Mr Bamford, Mr Curtis, Mr McMinn, and Mr Pepper, the last being in charge of JCB transport logistics and, at one time, their Dancing Digger display team, which performs worldwide.

Soon there was a hive of activity in the river, as the two tugs arrived to start their operations, plus other small workboats, one of which dropped off the pilot and tow master. We then adjourned to the lighthouse commissioners' lounge to sign off the formalities so as to complete the transfer of ownership, although I had to borrow from Andrew the token £1 mentioned in the sale agreement. In addition to this, there was another 'consideration', as the traditional commercial anonymity of such agreements requires. The only other thing of interest in the bill of sale was reference to *Britannia* acquiring all sixty-four shares in the vessel, this being the historical way the ownership of trading vessels was often split. This was to share the risk of the cargo, or the vessel itself, being lost at sea. Sitting at the commissioners' table over a cold buffet lunch, we reflected on just what we had accomplished – *Windsor Castle*, or rather *Fingal*, was finally ours!

Our joy was soon tempered by news that the port anchor had snagged. Observing a large, faraway buoy, holding the massive refrigerated cargo ship in place, bounce up and down soon told us what the problem was – the buoy's own anchor chain had been laid across *Windsor Castle*'s. After an hour or so of repeated efforts to lift the anchor, the decision to cut *Windsor Castle*'s anchor chain and secure it to a small buoy was made; we would have to send a boat back to collect it the following day. This decision was necessary primarily because we were running out of time: *Windsor Castle* was pointing up river and to turn her safely using the tugs required as much water as possible. The tide was due to turn against us shortly, narrowing the channel and giving the pilot some angst.

With *Windsor Castle* successfully turned around, we looked forward to a pleasant sail downriver to Falmouth. Alas, thick billowing smoke from the lead tug meant that we spent most of the journey looking back the other way. After several hours, we arrived at Falmouth docks and tied up at a disused berth on the outer wall, where *Windsor Castle* would remain until going into drydock for the insurance survey.

The following morning, we had an early start because we wanted to visit the Charlestown Shipwreck & Heritage Centre, an interesting diversion for us en route to Bristol airport and back home to Edinburgh. Little did I know that this lovely harbour was to star in the forthcoming *Poldark* television series.

In early August, our Derek Miller went back down to Cornwall to oversee the drydocking survey and, hopefully, the pre-tow works. Thankfully, the insurance survey reported that all was in good order and our attention now turned to *Fingal* coming home.

Leith's motto is 'Persevere', and, about 9.00 p.m. on Friday 22 August 2014, I witnessed *Fingal* arrive at the lock entrance into Leith, thus ending a process that originally started in December 2008.

CHAPTER 22

Prepare to be Dazzled!

In the First World War, British and Allied merchant shipping came under dire threat from the deadly predations of German U-boats, which were intent on severing the supply lifelines that were vital for survival and to help prosecute the war.

As a response, several thousands of these vulnerable vessels, together with a considerable number of warships, were subjected to visually 'disruptive' paint schemes. Their purpose was to confuse the enemy's ability to determine accurately the course and speed of a target when viewed through a submarine periscope, thereby making it more difficult to compute a firing solution for torpedo attack.

The adopted scheme, which became known as 'Dazzle', is credited to the celebrated British marine artist and illustrator Norman Wilkinson. In 1915, he began war service at sea in the Royal Naval Volunteer Reserve. Two years later, he began serving as lieutenant commander on a minesweeper, where he became all too aware of the threat from German submarines. It was during this time that his idea for dazzle materialised.

Wilkinson understood that it was impossible to conceal a ship from the sights of a U-boat commander. His radical proposal was that the extreme opposite was the answer. He developed a scheme that used bold shapes and violent contrasts of colour and tone, the purpose of which was to promote visual confusion. Intrigued by his ideas, the Admiralty eventually made Wilkinson the head of a new dazzle-camouflage section. He assembled a team of artists and model-makers at the Royal Academy of Arts in London. Hundreds of camouflage schemes were developed for ships large and small. Each side of the ship had a different pattern. Bold shapes at bow and stern broke up the vessel's form; angled lines suggested that distinctive smokestacks could be leaning in another direction; curves on the hull could be mistaken for the shape of the bow wave of a fast-moving ship.

Wilkinson appointed dock officers at ports around Britain, who supervised the painting of ships from the completed designs. In 1917, observers were astounded by harbours full of colourful ships. Rendered mostly monochrome in the black-and-white pictures of the day, their real colourful impact may yet be appreciated in the hundreds of model ships in the collection of the Imperial War Museum in London.

In the First World War, over 4,000 British merchant ships were painted in Dazzle, which was also applied to 400 naval vessels. Although a profusion of schemes was implemented, so many factors were involved that it was impossible to determine which were important. At the very least, Dazzle was a morale booster: crews reported feeling safer serving on such ships, despite the fact that its effectiveness was never objectively proven. Dazzle was also used in the Second World War, but to a lesser extent.

As part of the centenary of the First World War, the concept of Dazzle has been reapplied through modern interpretations to key vessels selected

As part of the process of applying the Dazzle scheme to *Fingal* the ship was painted overall with a grey undercoat, giving her a pseudo-naval appearance. (Ruth Armstrong Photography)

A computer-generated image depicts the Dazzle scheme applied to the starboard side of *Fingal*. In keeping with wartime tradition, a different scheme was devised for the port side. (Ciara Phillips. Production still from *Every Woman*. Image courtesy of the artist and Edinburgh Art Festival.)

from various parts of Britain. In Scotland, *Fingal* has been honoured for this special role. To realise this project, the Glasgow-based Canadian-Irish artist Ciara Phillips was commissioned in 2015. A Turner Prize finalist in 2014, Ciara is a graduate of Glasgow School of Art and works both individually and collaboratively, employing screen-printing, textile techniques and wall painting to create context-specific installations.

The 'Dazzled' *Fingal* forms part of the commemorations of the one-hundredth anniversary of the Battle of Jutland on 28 May 2016 and will be on display throughout the summer. Ultimately, *Fingal* will be painted in *Britannia* livery.

CHAPTER 23

Recollections of *Fingal*, by Shona McEachern

Shona McEachern is the daughter of *Fingal's* first Captain, and offers the following recollections of the ship:

I come from a long line of lighthouse personnel. My great-grandfather joined the NLB in the early 1860s as an assistant keeper and so began a long family association with the board, spanning three generations. My great-grandfather, grandfather, great-uncles, uncle and his cousins were all lighthouse keepers. Lighthouse families tended to marry within the lighthouse community, thus ever increasing the family span. Lighthouse names and those of their keepers were an ever-present part of growing up. My ancestors spent long years on the rock stations, particularly Dhu Heartach and Skerryvore. My grandfather was at the commissioning of the Flannan Isles lighthouse and was stationed there for several years immediately following the mysterious disappearance of the three lighthouse keepers in December 1900.

My father broke the mould when he joined the lighthouse tender *Pharos* in 1932 as an ordinary seaman, taking over from his older brother Archie, who had decided to follow the family tradition and head back to the lighthouses where he remained to become one of Scotland's longest-serving keepers.

FEBRUARY 2011:

A still, damp day on the River Fal in Cornwall. I follow the wooded path along the riverbank at Trelissick Gardens. As I turn each bend and gaze across the water, my excitement and sense of trepidation rises. Finally, I turn a corner, peer through a gap in the trees and bushes and, at last, catch a glimpse of my long-estranged friend and extended family member. There, amid the calm waters of Smugglers' Cove, a place in complete contrast to her earlier life riding Atlantic swells, sits *Fingal*.

For some time *Fingal* had been absent from my life, and I had spent a number of years trying to track her down. After trawling many websites, I had finally located her on the River Fal and went to view her there from afar on several occasions. Despite her having been repainted and renamed *Windsor Castle*, her distinctive beauty and elegant lines remained as always. Seeing *Fingal* once more, even given the strangeness of her surroundings, evoked many contrasting feelings and emotions, but the overriding ones were of relief and pleasure at seeing once more such an integral part of my formative years.

When rumours started to mount on social media that she had been moved from her berth on the River Fal, the big concern for her many followers was that she was about to be scrapped. I put in a plea asking if anyone knew what her fate was and, to my great relief, an anonymous response came back telling us not to worry, that she was in safe hands and going to a good home. It was only later that I discovered that the reassurance had come from none other than her new owners – the *Britannia* Trust!

PERSONAL RECOLLECTIONS:

I can't remember life before *Fingal*. I was two years old when, as a family, we relocated to Oban, awaiting her arrival. My father became her first Captain and was involved in her design at an early stage. As a child growing up in Oban, *Fingal* was ever-present in the household – a silent fifth member of the family. Evening meals were peppered with tales of her adventures that day and those of her crew. On arriving back in Oban from any time away, my gaze as I turned the corner and looked down the hill onto Oban Bay always fell upon the NLB pier to see if *Fingal* was home. It still does. My recollections arise from these memories and my own personal experiences. Like so many memories, it is as much about the sights, sounds and smells, which memory evokes as the actual words and tales themselves.

My walk home from primary school was about 2 miles in the opposite direction to Oban Bay. For a time, it became even longer as I set off, accompanied by a couple of friends, to visit *Fingal*. The idea behind this was apparently to get a lift home from school from my father, who left work at five o'clock. I remember on one occasion racing down the NLB pier, up the gangway and straight to the bow, where we proceeded to play among the ropes stored there. Great excitement! So much so that we were oblivious to the noise we were making and who we might be alerting to our uninvited presence. At some point I remember looking up and seeing a crew member glowering at us from a doorway. At the same time, a booming voice from above bellowed, 'what are you doing down there?' In terror, we dropped the ropes and looked up to see where the voice was coming from: just in time to see my father standing laughing, as he lowered the loudspeaker he had called us from. We didn't try that one again!

I used to go on trips on *Fingal*. On days when I considered the sea to be choppy, I can still hear my father saying, 'Sea! this is no sea!', so used was he and the crew to much more inclement conditions. On these occasions, when I started to feel the dreaded seasickness descend, my father would give me the wheel, tell me to keep my eyes focused on the horizon and that I was now responsible for steering the vessel. Of course, he was standing directly behind me, still totally in control. However, so intent was I on the task I had been assigned that the sickness was quickly forgotten. To this day, if I'm on a boat and the weather becomes rough, I still do this – minus the ship's wheel – and find it very effective.

The one outing that stands out from all the rest was our trip to visit the beautiful Skerryvore lighthouse, located 12 miles southwest of the island of Tiree. I was eight years old at the time and was joined by my cousin, three years my senior. It was a flat calm day in which we sighted a dead killer whale en route. As we approached the lighthouse, my father asked if we would like to go ashore and visit Skerryvore. Excited, and with some trepidation, we made our way down the pilot ladder to the boat below. At the light, my cousin was invited to ascend the 28 feet of ladder on the outside of the tower, which led to the entrance, in order to join the three keepers for tea and cake. At only eight years old, my father considered this too dangerous an ascent for me and so asked the crew, who were busy bringing water supplies onto the rock, to keep an eye on me. I was left sitting moodily throwing stones into a rock pool, as I watched the others ascend the steps and through the entrance into that beautiful tower.

The only time my father would arrive home from a spell at sea bearing material gifts was after a trip to the Isle of Man, where there were actually shops and things to buy! This would be the longest period of time he would be away – around ten days – and the family would gather around the wireless, tune into the appropriate frequency, and Dad would send us a message telling us his estimated time of arrival, so that tea would be ready for him on his return.

In the early hours of the morning of 15 January 1968, the shrill of the telephone had a hard job competing with the noise of the gale-force winds battering our home. My father dressed quickly and disappeared into that ghastly night, following the news that *Fingal* had broken her moorings and was adrift in Oban Bay. Thanks to her amazing night crew, the ship was finally secured and Dad returned home exhausted but very relieved. Having had a sleepless night, I was kept off school the next day. However, I was none too pleased on my return to find out that my class had been taken away from lessons on a trip to the seafront to see the devastation wreaked by the storm.

While *Fingal* was a large part of my life growing up, this interest extended to our wider family circle on both sides. For my mother's family living in north-west Scotland, *Fingal* was a welcome and much-loved sight. My mother's family home was on the west coast of Skye and one of my cousin's earliest memories is of *Fingal* arriving in Gesto Bay. He was then brought aboard the ship with his parents and siblings for refreshments. As the ship approached the Sound of Raasay, my father would blast the ship's whistle and my aunt, who lived in Raasay, would appear, brandishing a white tablecloth, which she used to wave in response.

My father was a raconteur. A particular tale that stands out for me centred around pay day. He described it thus:

> There was a cry: 'money overboard!' A seaman, clearing out the drawers in his cabin, accidentally threw his pay packet over the side.
>
> We were returning from the Isle of Man when I was informed this had happened and we were about 10 miles past the Mull of Kintyre, heading for the Sound of Islay at full speed of 14 knots. The wind was force five in an easterly direction. The crewman concerned had smoked one cigarette since the incident, so I reckoned that at least fifteen minutes had passed. What to do now? Was it worth turning back? Then I thought, if, after a night in the Isle of Man, he tells his wife he had thrown his pay over the side; will she believe him? I therefore turned the ship to starboard and ran back for fifteen minutes on a reciprocal course.
>
> Soon someone spotted paper in the sea so I stopped, lowered a boat and the second envelope picked up proved to be the missing money: £19. Fortunately, the loose change had previously been removed from the envelope. As this transpired, I had just finished discussing the matter with the Chief Officer and thought that I would need to 'pass the pot around', but we returned to Oban well satisfied.

The crew of *Fingal* were certainly a special breed, who worked hard in often treacherous conditions, but they were also intensely loyal and supportive of one another. I'm not the first to talk of the extended NLB family, who certainly appeared out of the woodwork to help our family in times of trouble.

Whenever I think of *Fingal*, it is of her making that elegant sail either in or out of Oban Bay. For me, that will forever be her spiritual home. While I have a strong attachment to *Fingal*, I am certainly not alone. The *Fingal* family extends far and wide. Like many, I would like to wish my old friend *Fingal* every success for a dazzling and exciting future.

Alongside at NLB pier, Oban, *Fingal* is passed by another local institution, the CalMac ferry *Isle of Mull*. (Author's Collection)

CHAPTER 24

Sister Lighthouse Authorities

The British Isles have three General Lighthouse Authorities: The Northern Lighthouse Board; Commissioners of Irish Lights; and Trinity House. They are jointly financed from 'light dues' levied on commercial shipping calling at ports within the areas of jurisdiction.

The Commissioners of Irish Lights is the General Lighthouse Authority for the whole of Ireland and its adjacent seas and islands. Trinity House is the authority for England, Wales, the Channel Islands and Gibraltar. As a Deep Sea Pilotage Authority, it licences certificated navigators to act as deep-sea pilots for ships trading in Northern European waters. Trinity House is also a charitable organisation dedicated to the safety, welfare and training of mariners.

The following images are contemporary with the operations of *Fingal*, in the 1990s:

ILV *Granuaile* attends the naming ceremony of the new RNLI lifeboat at Ballycotton. (Author's Collection)

Captain George Ball keeps ILV *Granuaile* close to the Coningbeg lightvessel during inspection. (Author's Collection)

Recovering the launches after attending Fastnet Rock lighthouse. (Author's Collection)

ILV *Granuaile* approaches the damaged Fundale buoy, prior to lifting aboard.
(Author's Collection)

Above: Connecting a buoy-lifting strop by launch. (Author's Collection)

Left: Lifting the Blackhall buoy aboard … (Author's Collection)

... and its mooring sinker. (Author's Collection)

Above: THV *Mermaid*: transferring a superstructure on the Morecambe High Focal Plane cardinal buoy. (Author's Collection)

Left: The author, as Second Officer on THV *Mermaid*, inspects and services the electrics on the Morecambe High Focal Plane buoy. (Author's Collection)

THV *Mermaid*: attending a blind (unlighted) buoy by launch in shallow water off Rhos-on-Sea, North Wales, for mooring replacement. (Author's Collection)

THV *Patricia* begins towing the East Goodwin lightvessel onto its assigned position. (Author's Collection)

THV *Mermaid:* transfer by helicopter to South Bishop lighthouse of operating fuel oil in under-slung pillow tanks. (Author's Collection)

Crew relief by helicopter from Cromer to the Dowsing lightvessel. The helicopter hovers until judged safe to land. (Author's Collection)

Above: THV *Patricia* approaches Dowsing lightvessel for scheduled replenishment and maintenance of moorings. (Author's Collection)

Left: Crew relief by helicopter from Cromer to the Dowsing lightvessel. (Author's Collection)

Right: Transfer of coal to the Dowsing lightvessel for the domestic heating boiler. (Author's Collection)

Below: Job done: Trinity House flagship *Patricia* departs. (Author's Collection)

CHAPTER 25

Fingal in those familiar places ...

At Stromness Depot.

At Oban Depot.

Negotiating the Sound of Kerrera, by Oban.

Overnight at the Small Vessel Anchorage, by Inchkeith, Firth of Forth.

Off Dunbar, in the approaches to the Firth of Forth.

The Tay, at Dundee.

At Stornoway, Isle of Lewis.

At Kyle of Lochalsh, near the Skye Bridge.

Approaching the Corran Narrows, near Fort William.

Loch Ryan, near Stranraer, south-west Scotland.

... by the light ...

Builder's Specification

TWIN-SCREW MOTOR VESSEL *FINGAL*

As Built
Owners: Northern Lighthouse Board
Builders: Blythswood Shipbuilding & Engineering Co. Ltd, Glasgow
Engine Builders: British Polar Engines Ltd, Govan, Glasgow
Machinery Installers: Aitchison Blair & Co., Clydebank
Date of Launch: 8 August 1963
Date of Trials: 19 December 1963
Trial Speed (mean): 15.25 knots
Moulded Dimensions
Length Overall: 237 feet, 8 inches
Breadth Overall: 40 feet, 4 inches
Draught (mean): 12 feet, 09 inches
Net Tonnage: 419 tons
Gross Tonnage: 1342 tons
Main Propulsion
Two Polar 2-stroke diesels, type M46M. Each engine has six cylinders, 960 bhp at 250 rpm. Engine-room control only.
Horse Power (combined): 1920bhp at 250 rpm

APPENDIX 2

Fingal's Programme, 1999

MARCH: Forth area buoys to service, 20 in total.
5 da (dissolved acetylene) to renew.
2 solar to renew (Stromness depot).
APRIL: Tay area buoys to service, 18 in total.
2 da to renew.
2 solar to renew (Stromness depot).
MAY: Moray Firth buoys to service, 17 in total.
2 da to renew.
3 solar to renew (Stromness depot).
JUNE: Minch buoys to service, 19 in total.
7 solar to renew (Oban depot).
JULY: Orkney & Shetland buoys to service, 27 in total.
5 solar to renew (Stromness depot).
2 solar OIC (Orkney Islands Council) to renew.
1 electric OIC to renew.
AUGUST: Clyde buoys to service, 22 in total.
5 solar to renew (Oban depot).
SEPTEMBER: Oban area buoys to service, 20 in total.
3 solar to renew (Oban depot).
OCTOBER: West coast unlit buoys to service, 19 in total.
9 to renew (Oban depot).
NOVEMBER: North and East unlit buoys to service, 9 in total.
1 to renew (Stromness depot).
ADDITIONAL: Oil rig inspections.
Drydock-refit.

APPENDIX 3

Passage Plan: Special Delivery

Ref.	Waypoint	Course	Distance	Distance to go
1	Oban: NLB Pier	Various	1.0	451.1
2	QG buoy; Kerrera Sound	210	2.2	450.1
3	Aird na Cuile	226	5.1	447.9
4	Insh Island	212	26.0	442.8
5	Rubh A'Mhail	204	4.0	416.8
6	Bunn'A'Bhainn	170	4.0	412.8
7	Am Meall	164	2.3	408.8
8	Fl.G.6s buoy	124	3.0	406.5
9	McArthurs Head	169	28.0	403.5
10	Mull of Kintyre	157	37.5	375.5
11	Mew Island	162	19.0	338.0
12	South Rock	188	156.0	319.0
13	Smalls TSS (N)	196	12.0	163.0
14	Smalls TSS (S)	181	91.0	151.0
15	Land's End TSS (N)	180	12.0	60.0
16	Land's End TSS (S)	110	6.5	48.0
17	Wolf Rock	088	24.5	41.5
18	Lizard Point	050	9.5	17.0
19	Manacles	000	4.0	7.5

Ref.	Waypoint	Course	Distance	Distance to go
20	Falmouth Pilot Station	352	3.5	3.5
21	St Anthony's Head			0.0

ESTIMATED TIMES OF ARRIVAL (450 NAUTICAL MILES) OBAN TO FALMOUTH PILOT STATION:

12 knots average: 37.5 hours
11 knots average: 41 hours
10 knots average: 45 hours

Acknowledgements

The author gratefully acknowledges with his thanks:

Bob Downie, CEO of RY *Britannia,* for recognising this book's potential and for realising its publication.

Captain Eric Smith NLB, for providing an authoritative introduction to set *Fingal* in her proper historical context: also for unstinting assistance in answering many queries.

Peter Wilson, Chief Engineer NLB (retired) for his insightful chapter concerning operations within the engineering department of *Fingal.*

Alan Provan NLB (retired) for the magnificent photograph on the front cover; also for additional information for the text.

Captain Sean Rathbone NLB.

Clinton Marwick NLB.

Lorna Hunter, NLB information officer, for valuable assistance from NLB headquarters, Edinburgh.

Captain Harry McClenahan, Commissioners of Irish Lights.

Jason James, of Marine & Towage Services, Falmouth.

Also to: Donald MacLeod, Shona McEachern, Crispin and Charlotte Worthington, Paul Robinson, John Ross, Ken Ross, Lawrence Macduff, Gordon Kent, Duncan Paul.

My wife Karen, for proofreading the text, providing computer expertise, and her full support in enabling this book to be written.